Shellfish

GENERAL EDITOR
CHUCK WILLIAMS

RECIPES
JOANNE WEIR

PHOTOGRAPHY
ALLAN ROSENBERG

TIME
LIFE
BOOKS

Time-Life Books is a division of
TIME LIFE INCORPORATED

President and CEO: John M. Fahey, Jr.
President, Time-Life Books: John D. Hall

TIME-LIFE CUSTOM PUBLISHING

Vice President and Publisher: Terry Newell
Sales Director: Frances C. Mangan
Editorial Director: Robert A. Doyle

WILLIAMS-SONOMA
Founder/Vice-Chairman: Chuck Williams

WELDON OWEN INC.
President: John Owen
Publisher: Wendely Harvey
Managing Editor: Laurie Wertz
Project Coordinator: Lisa Chaney Atwood
Consulting Editor: Norman Kolpas
Copy Editor: Sharon Silva
Design/Editorial Assistant: Janique Gascoigne
Design: John Bull, The Book Design Company
Production: Stephanie Sherman, James Obata
Food Photographer: Allan Rosenberg
Additional Food Photography: Allen V. Lott
Primary Food & Prop Stylist: Sandra Griswold
Food Stylist: Heidi Gintner
Assistant Food Stylist: Danielle Di Salvo
Glossary Illustrations: Alice Harth

The Williams-Sonoma Kitchen Library
conceived and produced by Weldon Owen Inc.
814 Montgomery St., San Francisco, CA 94133

In collaboration with Williams-Sonoma
100 North Point, San Francisco, CA 94133

Production by Mandarin Offset, Hong Kong
Printed in China

A Note on Weights and Measures:
All recipes include customary U.S. and metric
measurements. Metric conversions are based on
a standard developed for these books and have
been rounded off. Actual weights may vary.

A Weldon Owen Production

Copyright © 1995 Weldon Owen Inc.
All rights reserved, including the right of
reproduction in whole or in part in any form.

Library of Congress
Cataloging-in-Publication Data:

Weir, Joanne.
    Shellfish / general editor, Chuck Williams ;
recipes, Joanne Weir ; photography, Allan Rosenberg.
        p.   cm. — (Williams-Sonoma kitchen library)
    Includes index.
    ISBN 0-7835-0305-9
    1. Cookery (Shellfish)   I. Williams, Chuck.   II. Title.
III. Series.
TX753.W45   1995
641.6'94—dc20   94-3483
                                        CIP

Contents

Soups & Salads 15

First Courses 43

Main Courses 69

INTRODUCTION

I grew up along a tidal river in northern Florida, where we'd often go out and gather shrimp, oysters and clams for our dinner. People fortunate enough to live near clean ocean waters can still do that. But even those of us who now must go to a market for our shellfish share some of the satisfaction felt by those who harvest them for free: that of enjoying edible treasures from the sea.

This book celebrates shellfish in all their variety, including 45 recipes that feature—in words and full-color photographs—the most popular and readily available types: lobster, crab, shrimp, scallops, clams, mussels and oysters. It begins with an overview of the fundamentals of shellfish cookery, with guides to the equipment you may need and step-by-step instructions on how to clean and prepare fresh shellfish, as well as extract their delicious meat. Following the recipes is an illustrated glossary that defines major ingredients and basic techniques. In short, every page of this book is designed to give new inspiration to cooks who already love shellfish, and to encourage those who aren't as familiar with them to discover how easy and exciting cooking shellfish can be.

To both groups, however, I'd like to emphasize one important concern: freshness. Be sure to buy your shellfish from the most reputable merchant in your area—one who carries only the freshest, in-season shellfish and who has a brisk turnover of product. Before purchase, check all shellfish to make sure they are alive (or, in the case of precooked lobsters or crabs, are perfectly fresh); that they have only the fresh, clean scent of the sea; and that they are otherwise free of any signs of poor handling. Don't be afraid to ask questions about the shellfish, and if you're left with any doubts whatsoever, don't buy it.

Follow my advice and you're sure to get only shellfish in peak condition. Let this book become your guide to cooking and enjoying them at their finest.

Chuck Williams

EQUIPMENT

An array of cookware and tools simplifies the preparation of shellfish recipes

Well-stocked kitchens will already contain much of the equipment necessary to cook shellfish. Anyone interested in shellfish cookery, however, should make a few small investments in specialized equipment. An oyster knife, for example, opens that prized shellfish—as well as clams—more efficiently than any other blade. And an array of tools—mallet, pick and cracker—makes it easy to remove every last morsel of precious meat from crabs and lobsters.

1. Stockpot
Tall, deep, large-capacity pot with close-fitting lid, for making stock or for steaming or simmering whole lobsters, crabs or large quantities of smaller shellfish. Select a good-quality, heavy pot that absorbs and transfers heat well.

2. Saucepan
For simmering stock and sauces and for cooking small shellfish stews and braises.

3. Liquid Measuring Cup
For accurate measuring of liquid ingredients. Choose heavy-duty heat-resistant glass, marked on one side in cups and ounces, on the other in milliliters. Lip and handle allow for easy pouring.

4. Strainer
Fine-mesh stainless steel, for straining solids from stock or removing shellfish from simmering liquids.

5. Chef's Knife
Large, all-purpose knife for cutting lobster, as well as for general chopping and slicing of ingredients.

6. Paring Knife
For peeling vegetables and cutting up small ingredients.

7. Scrubbing Brush
Sturdy brush with stiff bristles, for cleaning the shells of bivalves and mollusks.

8. Mallet
Sturdy wooden mallet with metal-reinforced striking surfaces, for cracking the hard shells of cooked lobsters and crabs.

9. Skewers
For holding small pieces of shellfish during grilling or broiling. Before using, soak wooden or bamboo skewers in water for 30 minutes to prevent burning.

10. Kitchen Shears
All-purpose high-carbon-steel shears with one serrated edge for efficient cutting of fairly soft ingredients or for cutting through softer parts of crab or lobster shells.

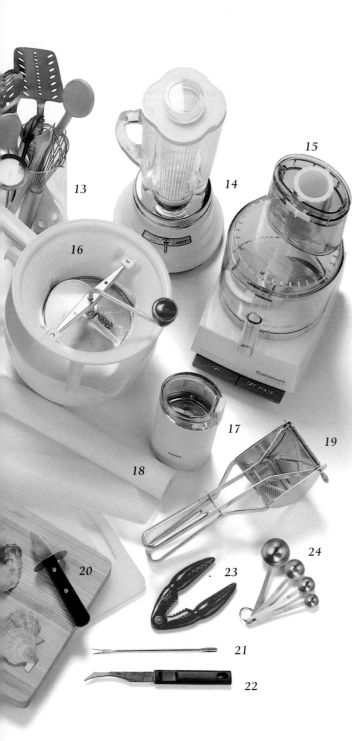

11. Cheesecloth
For straining fine particles from seafood stock or from liquids in which shellfish have simmered or steamed. Muslin may also be used.

12. Mortar and Pestle
For crushing garlic or small quantities of other seasonings.

13. Assorted Kitchen Tools
Glass jar holds slotted spatula and slotted spoon for lifting and draining simmered shellfish; wooden spoons for all-purpose mixing and stirring; tongs for retrieving hot shellfish and arranging final presentations; small wire whisk for mixing ingredients and stirring sauces; and deep-frying thermometer.

14. Electric Blender
For rapid blending of sauces and puréeing of relatively small quantities of ingredients.

15. Food Processor
For general preparation of ingredients in large quantities, and for rapid puréeing or blending of sauces.

16. Food Mill
Hand-cranked mill purées ingredients by forcing them through its conical grinding disk, which also sieves out pieces of shell, fibers, skins and seeds. Most models include both medium and fine disks for coarser or smoother purées.

17. Electric Grinder
For quickly and easily grinding larger quantities of whole spices, use a small electric mill such as the coffee mill shown here. Dedicate one mill to spices, to prevent coffee and spice flavors from mingling.

18. Parchment Paper
Sturdy, heatproof, stick-resistant paper can be used to wrap shellfish for oven baking *en papillote*—"in an envelope."

19. Ricer
Sturdy, hinged stainless-steel apparatus forces boiled potatoes and other soft ingredients through small holes, producing fine-textured, smooth purées.

20. Oyster Knife
Short, sturdy pointed blade designed to be wedged between the halves of an oyster's shell and then twisted to force it open. Curved blade edge then cuts beneath the oyster to detach it from the shell.

21. Lobster Pick
Slender stainless-steel pick with forked end, for inserting into the shell crevices of lobsters—and crabs—to extract the meat.

22. Shrimp Deveining Knife
Curved, tapered stainless-steel blade slices through a shrimp's shell and strips out its intestinal vein in a single motion.

23. Lobster Cracker
Heavy, hinged metal cracker firmly grips and breaks the hard claw and leg shells of lobsters and crabs.

24. Measuring Spoons
In graduated sizes, for measuring small quantities of ingredients. Select good-quality calibrated metal spoons with deep bowls.

Cleaning and Cracking Cooked Lobster

Whether you cook a lobster yourself or buy it already cooked, its meat may be extracted fairly easily following these instructions. To keep the tail meat whole, twist off the tail section from the body; then carefully cut through the shell's thinner underside and pry it open to reveal the tail meat.

3. Removing the body meat.
Pull out and discard the black vein that runs the length of the body meat, as well as the small sand sac at the base of the head. Remove the white meat from the shell. If you like, reserve the green tomalley (the liver) and any coral-colored roe, which can be added to lobster dishes for extra flavor.

1. Draining the excess water.
Drain any residual water from boiled or steamed lobsters by making a small cut between the eyes on the lobster head. Hold the lobster by its tail over a sink to drain the excess cooking liquid from underneath the shell.

4. Removing the tail meat.
Firmly grasp the fins of a tail half with one hand. With the other hand, firmly pull out the tail meat in a single piece. Repeat with the other tail half.

2. Halving the lobster.
Insert the tip of a large, sharp, sturdy knife into the point where the tail and body sections meet, and carefully cut through the tail. Turn the lobster around and continue to cut from the center through the head, cutting the lobster into two equal halves.

5. Cracking the claws.
Firmly twist off the claws from the body shells. With a lobster cracker or mallet, break the hard shell of each claw in several places. Pull away the shell pieces, taking care not to damage the claw meat if a recipe calls for it to be left whole.

CLEANING AND CRACKING COOKED CRAB

Nowadays, most seafood shops sell fresh whole crabs already cooked. But, to ensure the best results in any recipe that calls for crab, it is important to ask for and insist on cooked crabs that have not been frozen after cooking. Frozen crab lacks the sweetness, moistness and firm texture found in fresh crab.

Although many stores sell crab meat already extracted from the shell, the meat will be more flavorful—and economical—if you extract it yourself, following the instructions shown here. The steps may look confusing at first, but once you've done the job a few times it will become quite easy.

3. Cleaning the crab.
Pull or scrape out the dark gray intestines from the center of the body, along with any orange roe you might find. Scrape and rinse out the top shell if it is to be used in the recipe's presentation.

4. Removing the gills.
Using a spoon or your fingers, scrape or pull off and discard the spongy, feather-shaped white gills on either side of the crab's body.

1. Removing the apron.
Using your hands, twist off the crab's legs and claws and set them aside. Turn the crab upside down and, using your thumb or the tip of a short, sturdy knife, pry off the small, triangular apron-shaped shell flap.

5. Removing the meat.
Using your hands, break the crab's body in half to reveal the meat. Using your fingers, a knife or a lobster pick, remove the meat from all the body cavities.

2. Removing the top shell.
Insert your thumbs in the small crevice between the underside of the crab's body and its top shell. Pull them apart, lifting the top shell away from the body.

6. Cracking the claws and legs.
Using a mallet or lobster cracker, crack the shells of the claws in several places, as well as any legs large enough to contain a good amount of meat. Break away the shell pieces and remove the meat with your fingers or a lobster pick.

Cleaning and Shucking Oysters

Whether served raw on the half shell (page 43) or cooked, fresh oysters should be bought alive and only from the most reputable seafood merchants. Their shells should be tightly closed—or close quickly when handled—and their only aroma should be a fresh, clean ocean scent. Although the rule that you can eat oysters safely only during months with the letter "r" in them is a myth, they'll be at their best in autumn and winter. Many shops will open, or shuck, oysters for you. But, to enjoy them at their freshest, it is best to open them just before use—a somewhat arduous task that can nonetheless be mastered by dedicated oyster lovers.

1. Scrubbing the oyster.
Discard any oysters that smell bad or whose shells are open. Using a stiff-bristled kitchen brush, thoroughly scrub the shell of each oyster, rinsing it under cold running water.

2. Opening the shell.
During shucking, protect your hand from the sharp-edged shell by gripping the oyster flat-side up with a folded kitchen towel. To one side of the hinge, opposite the shell's concentric ridges, push in the tip of an oyster knife and pry upward to open the shell.

3. Cutting the shell free.
Keeping the blade edge against the inside of the top shell, run the knife all around the oyster to cut the muscle that holds the shell halves together. Lift off and discard the top shell.

4. Detaching the oyster.
Run the knife underneath the oyster to cut its flesh free from the bottom shell. Reserve the oyster liquor (liquid) in the bottom shell if it is required in the recipe.

Debearding and Cleaning Mussels

1. Debearding the mussel.
Firmly grasp the fibrous beard attached to the edge of each mussel and pull it off. Check all the mussels carefully, discarding those whose shells are not tightly closed.

2. Cleaning the mussel.
Rinse the mussels thoroughly under cold running water. One at a time, hold them under the water and scrub with a stiff-bristled brush to remove any stubborn dirt.

PEELING AND DEVEINING SHRIMP

Raw shrimp (prawns) are generally sold with the heads removed but the shells intact. Before cooking, they are usually peeled and their veinlike intestinal tracts removed using the method shown here or the deveining knife shown on page 7. After deveining, large shrimp may be butterflied so they cook more evenly.

Most raw shrimp for sale today are, in fact, flash frozen at the time of the catch, and may develop a slight smell reminiscent of ammonia by the time they reach your store. To freshen them, soak them in salted water for 10–15 minutes (after peeling and deveining), using 1 teaspoon salt in a bowl filled with enough cold water to cover the shellfish. Drain and rinse well in fresh water before using.

1. Splitting the shell.
Using your fingers, split open the shrimp's thin shell along the concave side, between its two rows of legs.

2. Peeling the shrimp.
Peel away the shell. If a recipe calls for it, take care to leave the last segment with tail fin intact and attached to the shrimp meat.

3. Exposing the vein.
Using a small, sharp knife, carefully make a shallow slit along the peeled shrimp's back, just deep enough to expose the long, usually dark, veinlike intestinal tract.

4. Deveining the shrimp.
With the tip of the knife or your fingers, lift up and pull out the vein, discarding it.

If a recipe calls for butterflying the shrimp, slit down into the meat just far enough so that, with your fingertips, you can open it out and flatten it easily into two equal-sized lobes.

PREPARING CLAMS

1. Testing for freshness.
Fresh live clams—as well as oysters and mussels—will have tightly closed shells. If one gapes open, pick it up: The shell should quickly close tight. If it doesn't, discard the clam.

2. Scrubbing the clam.
As a further test, put the clams in a container filled with water; discard any that do not sink to the bottom. Then scrub each clam thoroughly with a stiff-bristled brush.

Fish Stock

The best fish bones to use for stock are those from snapper, grouper, cod, perch, sole, trout, pike or salmon. Be sure to simmer the stock for only 40 minutes, to retain its sweet flavor. Leftover stock can be frozen for up to 2 months.

2–2½ lb (1–1.25 kg) fish skeletons with
    some meat attached
1 cup (8 fl oz/250 ml) dry white wine
1 small yellow onion, coarsely chopped
1 small carrot, coarsely chopped
12 fresh parsley stems
pinch of fresh or dried thyme
1 bay leaf

Remove gills, fat, skin, tail and any traces of blood from the fish bones. Rinse the bones and place in a stockpot. Add water to the level of the bones. Then add the wine to cover the fish bones completely. Finally, add all the remaining ingredients.

Bring to a boil, reduce the heat to low and simmer, uncovered, for 40 minutes. During cooking, use a wooden spoon to crush the bones occasionally.

Remove from the heat and pour immediately through a fine-mesh sieve lined with cheesecloth (muslin) into a clean vessel. Run a spoon over the surface to scoop up any fat, or place a paper towel over the surface and then lift it off to remove the fat. Use immediately, or cover and refrigerate for up to 3 days or freeze for up to 2 months.

*Makes about 5 cups
(40 fl oz/1.25 l)*

1. Rinsing the fish bones.
After removing gills, fat, skin and tails, put the fish bones in a colander or sieve and rinse well under cold running water. Add to a stockpot with water, wine and other ingredients and bring to a boil.

2. Straining the stock.
Simmer the stock, uncovered, for about 40 minutes, occasionally breaking up the bones with a wooden spoon. Immediately strain through a fine-mesh sieve lined with cheesecloth (muslin) set above a clean container large enough to hold the stock.

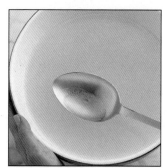

3. Skimming the stock.
Using a spoon, skim off any fat from the surface of the stock; or drape a paper towel on its surface briefly, then lift it off. Use immediately, or cover and refrigerate or freeze.

Quick Fish Stock

If you get into a bind and don't have any fish bones, fish stock, or time, this simple stock is the next best thing.

1 cup (8 fl oz/250 ml) dry white wine
2 cups (16 fl oz/500 ml) bottled clam juice
2 cups (16 fl oz/500 ml) water
½ yellow onion, coarsely chopped
½ carrot, peeled and coarsely chopped
6 fresh parsley stems
pinch of fresh or dried thyme
1 bay leaf

In a saucepan, combine all the ingredients and bring to a boil. Reduce the heat to low and simmer, uncovered, for 20 minutes. Remove from the heat and strain through a fine-mesh sieve. Use immediately, or cover and refrigerate for up to 3 days or freeze for up to 2 months.

Makes about 4 cups (32 fl oz/1 l)

Court Bouillon

Cooking crabs, lobsters and other shellfish in this delicate, fragrant liquid enhances their individual flavors.

8 cups (64 fl oz/2 l) water
1 bottle (3 cups/24 fl oz/750 ml) dry white wine
2 carrots, peeled and coarsely chopped
2 yellow onions, coarsely chopped
6 fresh parsley stems
pinch of fresh or dried thyme
4 bay leaves
10 peppercorns
1 tablespoon salt

In a stockpot, combine all the ingredients and bring to a boil. Reduce the heat to low and simmer, uncovered, for 40 minutes. Remove from the heat and strain through a fine-mesh sieve. Use immediately, or cover and refrigerate for up to 1 week or freeze for up to 2 months.

Makes about 8 cups (64 fl oz/2 l) .

Mayonnaise

Creamy mayonnaise is a natural complement to the subtle flavor of shellfish. To make the preparation of mayonnaise a bit easier, have all the ingredients at room temperature. It can also be made in a blender or in a small food processor. Use the same basic method, adding the oil in a thin, steady stream while the motor is running.

1 egg yolk
1 teaspoon Dijon mustard
⅓ cup (3 fl oz/80 ml) olive oil
⅓ cup (3 fl oz/80 ml) safflower oil or peanut oil
juice of ½ lemon
salt and freshly ground pepper

In a bowl, whisk together the egg yolk, mustard and 1 tablespoon of the olive oil until an emulsion forms. Combine the remaining olive oil and the safflower or peanut oil in a pitcher. Drop by drop and whisking constantly, add 2–3 tablespoons of the oil to the egg yolk mixture. Once the mixture thickens, add the remaining oil in a very thin, steady stream, whisking constantly, until all of the oil has been incorporated.

Stir in the lemon juice and salt and pepper to taste. Cover and store in the refrigerator for up to 1 week.

*Makes about 1 cup
(8 fl oz/250 ml)*

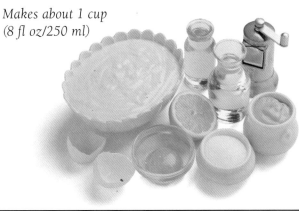

Gazpacho with Shrimp

1 cup (8 fl oz/250 ml) fish stock or quick fish stock (recipes on pages 12–13) or bottled clam juice

½ lb (250 g) medium shrimp (prawns), peeled and deveined

3 cups (18 oz/560 g) peeled, halved, seeded and chopped tomatoes (fresh or canned)

1 green bell pepper (capsicum), seeded, deribbed and coarsely chopped

1 red (Spanish) onion, coarsely chopped

1 large cucumber, peeled, halved, seeded and coarsely chopped

5–6 tablespoons (2½–3 fl oz/80–90 ml) red wine vinegar

3 large cloves garlic, minced

1¼ cups (10 fl oz/310 ml) tomato juice

¼ cup (2 fl oz/60 ml) extra-virgin olive oil

1 slice coarse-textured white bread, crust removed, soaked in water to cover for 10 seconds and squeezed dry

salt and freshly ground pepper

FOR THE GARNISH:

1 tablespoon olive oil

1 tablespoon unsalted butter

3 cloves garlic, crushed

6 slices coarse-textured white bread, crusts removed, cut into small cubes

¼ cup (1½ oz/45 g) finely diced green bell pepper (capsicum)

¼ cup (1½ oz/45 g) peeled, halved, seeded and finely diced cucumber

½ tomato, finely diced

¼ cup (1½ oz/45 g) finely diced red (Spanish) onion

In Spain, there are dozens of varieties of gazpacho, the icy cold liquid salad that is a refreshing antidote to the heat of summer. This terrific version can be made with scallops in place of shrimp. If you like, serve the soup in chilled bowls to keep it cold.

❋

*I*n a frying pan, bring the fish stock or clam juice to a boil. Add the shrimp, reduce the heat to low, cover and simmer for 1 minute. Uncover, stir lightly, re-cover and simmer until the shrimp curl and are firm to the touch, 1 minute longer. Using a slotted spoon, transfer the shrimp to a bowl. Cover the shrimp and broth and refrigerate separately until cool.

In a large bowl, stir together the cooled cooking liquid, tomatoes, bell pepper, onion, cucumber, 5 tablespoons (2½ fl oz/80 ml) vinegar, garlic, tomato juice, olive oil and bread. Working in batches, purée in a blender on high speed until very smooth, 3–4 minutes. Pass the purée through a coarse-mesh sieve into another large bowl. Season to taste with salt, pepper and vinegar. Chop the shrimp coarsely. Stir it into the purée, cover and refrigerate until well chilled, about 3 hours.

To prepare the garnish, in a frying pan over medium-low heat, warm the olive oil and butter. Add the garlic and sauté, stirring, until golden brown, about 1 minute. Remove the garlic and discard. Add the bread cubes and stir to coat with the oil and butter. Sauté over medium heat, stirring occasionally, until the bread cubes are golden, about 10 minutes. Transfer the croutons to a plate and let cool.

To serve, ladle the soup into bowls. Garnish with the diced bell pepper, cucumber, tomato, onion and croutons.

Serves 6

Poached Shrimp and Scallop Salad with Mango Salsa

½ cup (4 fl oz/125 ml) fish stock or quick fish stock (*recipes on pages 12–13*) or bottled clam juice

¾ lb (375 g) medium or large shrimp (prawns), peeled and deveined

¾ lb (375 g) sea or bay scallops

2 large, ripe mangoes

½ red bell pepper (capsicum), seeded, deribbed and cut into ¼-inch (6-mm) dice

1 fresh jalapeño chili pepper, seeded and minced (optional)

1 teaspoon grated lime zest

juice of 2–3 limes

3 tablespoons chopped fresh mint leaves, plus mint sprigs for garnish

2 tablespoons extra-virgin olive oil

salt and freshly ground pepper

lime wedges

This fruit-and-shellfish combination is an ideal luncheon salad. If you like, substitute 1 small papaya for the mangoes. To prepare the papaya, peel and seed it, then cut the flesh into ½-inch (12-mm) dice.

In a frying pan, bring the fish stock or clam juice to a boil. Add the shrimp, reduce the heat to low, cover and simmer for 1 minute. Stir lightly, re-cover and cook until the shrimp curl and are firm to the touch, about 1 minute for medium shrimp and 2 minutes for large shrimp. Using a slotted spoon, transfer the shrimp to a bowl.

If you are using sea scallops, cut them horizontally into slices ¼ inch (6 mm) thick. Leave bay scallops whole. Add the scallops to the same simmering liquid, then cover and simmer until almost firm to the touch, about 2 minutes, turning the sea scallops halfway through the cooking process. Using a slotted spoon, transfer to the bowl holding the shrimp. Cover and refrigerate. Discard the cooking liquid.

Working with 1 mango at a time, cut off the flesh lengthwise from each side of the large, flat mango pit, to form 2 large pieces. Discard the pit. Using a knife, score the flesh lengthwise and then crosswise through to the skin. Now slip the blade between the skin and the flesh and cut away the flesh (which will be in small cubes), dropping it into a bowl.

Add to the bowl the bell pepper, jalapeño pepper, lime zest, lime juice, chopped mint, olive oil and salt and pepper to taste. Mix well. Add the shrimp and scallops and toss gently.

Place on a platter. Garnish with mint sprigs and serve with lime wedges.

Serves 6

Mussels Provençale

3 lb (1.5 kg) mussels, debearded and
  well scrubbed
½ cup (4 fl oz/125 ml) dry white wine
1 small yellow onion, chopped
3 cloves garlic, coarsely chopped, plus
  2 cloves garlic, minced
6 fresh parsley stems, plus ⅓ cup
  (½ oz/15 g) chopped fresh parsley,
  preferably flat-leaf (Italian)
pinch of fresh or dried thyme
1 bay leaf
3–4 tablespoons fresh lemon juice
½ cup (4 fl oz/125 ml) extra-virgin
  olive oil
salt and freshly ground pepper
lemon wedges

Clams can be substituted for the mussels in this simple yet flavorful dish from Provence. Serve with a good crusty French bread, for soaking up all the tasty juices.

✽

Discard any mussels that do not close to the touch. In a saucepan, bring the wine to a boil. Add the mussels, onion, coarsely chopped garlic, parsley stems, thyme and bay leaf. Reduce the heat to medium, cover and simmer, shaking the pan periodically, until the mussels open, 2–4 minutes. Using a slotted spoon, transfer the mussels to a large bowl and let cool. Discard any unopened mussels.

Strain the cooking liquid through a sieve lined with several layers of cheesecloth (muslin) or a coffee filter into a small, clean saucepan. Reduce the liquid over high heat by half to about ½ cup (4 fl oz/125 ml). Let cool.

In a small bowl, whisk together the lemon juice, olive oil, minced garlic, reduced cooking liquid and salt and pepper to taste.

Add the dressing and the chopped parsley to the mussels and toss well. Transfer to a platter. Garnish with lemon wedges and serve.

Serves 6

Lobster and Fava Bean Salad

7 cups (56 fl oz/1.75 l) water or court
  bouillon (recipe on page 13)
salt
2 live lobsters, about 1¼ lb (625 g) each
4 lb (2 kg) young, tender fava (broad)
  beans in the shell
½ small head romaine (cos) lettuce,
  tender leaves only, carefully washed,
  dried and cut crosswise into strips
  ½ inch (12 mm) wide (optional)
¼ cup (2 fl oz/60 ml) fresh orange juice
1 tablespoon balsamic vinegar
½ teaspoon finely grated orange zest
½ cup (4 fl oz/125 ml) extra-virgin
  olive oil
1 clove garlic, minced
2 tablespoons chopped fresh parsley
salt and freshly ground pepper
orange wedges (optional)

The vibrant green fava beans contrast beautifully with the coral lobster meat in this dazzling salad. If there are no young and tender fava beans in the market, substitute 1 pound (500 g) asparagus or green beans. Trim them, cut on the diagonal into ¾-inch (2-cm) pieces and simmer in salted water to cover until tender-crisp, about 5 minutes.

❁

*I*n a stockpot, bring the water or court bouillon to a boil. If using water, add 1 tablespoon salt once it boils. Add the lobsters and cook until dark red and fully cooked, about 10 minutes. Using tongs, remove the lobsters from the pot and set aside to cool. Discard the cooking liquid.

When the lobsters are cool, remove the meat from the tails and claws as directed on page 8. Reserve body meat for other uses. Dice the tail and claw meat into ½-inch (12-mm) pieces and place in a large salad bowl. Set aside.

Remove the tough outer pods from the fava beans. Fill a saucepan three-fourths full of water and bring to a boil. Add the fava beans and boil for 30 seconds. Drain and let cool. Remove the thin skin covering each bean by making a small slit in the skin and then popping out the tender bean. Discard the skins. Add the fava beans to the bowl holding the lobster, along with the lettuce, if using.

In a small bowl, whisk together the orange juice, vinegar, orange zest, olive oil, garlic, parsley and salt and pepper to taste.

Add the dressing to the bowl holding the lobster and toss well. Place on a platter and garnish with orange wedges, if desired. Serve immediately.

Serves 6

fur

Fennel, Celery and Oyster Soup

18 small oysters in the shell or drained
   bottled shucked oysters
3 large fennel bulbs, with stems and
   feathery tops intact
3 tablespoons unsalted butter
1 yellow onion, coarsely chopped
3 celery stalks, coarsely chopped
3 cups (24 fl oz/750 ml) fish stock or
   quick fish stock (*recipes on pages 12–13*)
   or bottled clam juice
2 cups (16 fl oz/500 ml) water
salt and freshly ground pepper
½ cup (4 fl oz/125 ml) heavy (double)
   cream
1–2 teaspoons fresh lemon juice

*There is an appealing delicacy to this creamy soup. If you like,
substitute 6 leeks, including 3 inches (7.5 cm) of the tender green
tops, carefully washed and chopped, for the fennel and celery.*

❋

*I*f using oysters in the shell, shuck them as directed on page 10,
reserving their liquor. Refrigerate the oysters; set the liquor aside.

   Cut off the feathery tops from the fennel bulbs and set aside.
Remove the stalks and any tough or bruised outer leaves from
the bulbs and discard. Coarsely chop 2 of the fennel bulbs.

   In a soup pot over medium heat, melt 2 tablespoons of the
butter. Add the onion and sauté until soft, about 10 minutes.
Add the chopped fennel, celery, fish stock or clam juice, water
and fresh oyster liquor. Bring to a boil, reduce the heat to
medium-low, and simmer uncovered until the vegetables are
very soft, about 30 minutes. Let cool slightly.

   Purée in a blender until very smooth, 3–4 minutes. Pass the
purée through a fine-mesh sieve into a clean saucepan. Set aside.

   Using a sharp knife, cut the remaining fennel bulb into paper-
thin slices. In a frying pan over low heat, melt the remaining
1 tablespoon butter. Add the sliced fennel, cover and cook,
stirring occasionally, until soft yet still slightly crisp, about 10
minutes. Season to taste with salt and pepper.

   Place the purée over medium heat. Add the cream, oysters and
sautéed fennel. Bring to a gentle simmer and simmer uncovered
until the oysters are cooked, 1–2 minutes; they should be
slightly firm to the touch. Add the lemon juice to taste.

   Chop the reserved fennel tops. Ladle the soup into warmed
bowls. Sprinkle with the fennel tops and serve immediately.

Serves 6

Italian Shellfish Salad with Salsa Verde

½ cup (4 fl oz/125 ml) fish stock or quick fish stock (*recipes on pages 12–13*), bottled clam juice or water

½ lb (250 g) medium shrimp (prawns)

½ lb (250 g) sea or bay scallops

2 lb (1 kg) mussels, debearded and well scrubbed

2 lb (1 kg) clams, well scrubbed

½ cup (¾ oz/20 g) chopped fresh parsley

4 tablespoons chopped fresh chives

½ teaspoon chopped fresh thyme

½ teaspoon chopped fresh oregano

2 tablespoons well-drained capers, chopped

2 anchovy fillets, soaked in cold water to cover for 5 minutes, drained, patted dry and mashed

2 cloves garlic, minced

4–5 tablespoons (2–2½ fl oz/60–75 ml) fresh lemon juice

½ cup (4 fl oz/125 ml) extra-virgin olive oil

salt and freshly ground pepper

lemon wedges

Each seaside village along Italy's Amalfi coast makes its own distinctive version of this shellfish salad. Serve the salad within 1 hour of making it, or the lemon juice will discolor the herbs. Pass grilled Italian bread rubbed with garlic for dipping into the juices.

❋

*I*n a frying pan over medium heat, bring the fish stock, clam juice or water to a boil. Add the shrimp and scallops, reduce the heat to low, cover and simmer until almost firm to the touch, 1–2 minutes. Using a slotted spoon, transfer the shrimp and scallops to a large bowl and let cool.

Discard any mussels and clams that do not close to the touch. Add the mussels to the same simmering liquid, cover and cook, shaking the pan periodically, until they open, 2–4 minutes. Using a slotted spoon, lift out the mussels as they open and set aside. Discard any unopened mussels. Cook the clams in the same way until they open, 3–5 minutes, and remove them as well. Discard any unopened clams. Reduce the cooking liquid over high heat to 2 tablespoons and remove from the heat.

Peel the shrimp and devein. Return to the bowl holding the scallops. Remove all but 6 mussels and 6 clams from their shells and add the shelled and unshelled mussels and clams to the shrimp and scallops. Add the reduced cooking liquid to the shellfish and toss to coat evenly.

In a bowl, whisk together the parsley, chives, thyme, oregano, capers, anchovy, garlic, lemon juice and olive oil. Whisk in salt and pepper to taste. Pour the dressing over the shellfish, toss well and let stand for 30 minutes.

Place the shellfish on a platter and garnish with lemon wedges. Serve immediately.

Serves 6

Warm Scallop and Asparagus Salad with Orange Dressing

3 large navel oranges

½ teaspoon peeled and grated fresh ginger

3 tablespoons balsamic vinegar

½ teaspoon Asian sesame oil

6 tablespoons (3 fl oz/90 ml) olive oil

salt and freshly ground pepper

1 tablespoon sesame seeds

1 lb (500 g) asparagus, trimmed and cut on the diagonal into 1½-inch (4-cm) lengths

1½ lb (750 g) sea scallops, cut horizontally into slices ½ inch (12 mm) thick

Substitute thinly sliced green (spring) onions or slivers of crisply fried fresh ginger for the sesame seed garnish, if you prefer.

❋

Holding 1 orange over a small bowl, grate enough zest to measure 1 teaspoon. Then cut the orange in half crosswise and add the juice of one-half of the orange to the bowl. Set aside the remaining half. Add the ginger, vinegar, sesame oil, 4 table-spoons (2 fl oz/60 ml) of the olive oil and salt and pepper to taste to the bowl. Stir well and set aside.

Using a sharp knife, cut the tops and bottoms off the remaining 2 whole oranges and the top off the reserved orange half to reveal the flesh. Trim all the peel so that no white pith remains. Cut the oranges crosswise into slices ¼ inch (6 mm) thick. Discard any seeds, then cut the slices in half. Set aside.

In a small, dry frying pan over medium heat, toast the sesame seeds until golden, about 1 minute. Set aside.

Fill a saucepan three-fourths full of water and bring to a boil. Add salt to taste and the asparagus and boil uncovered until tender-crisp, about 5 minutes. Drain well and set aside.

In a frying pan over high heat, warm 1 tablespoon of the olive oil. Add half of the scallops and sauté, stirring occasionally, until almost firm to the touch, 2–3 minutes. Season with salt and pepper. Transfer to a plate. Cook the remaining scallops in the same way, using the remaining 1 tablespoon olive oil.

Return the first batch of scallops to the pan, along with the dressing and asparagus. Warm gently, stirring occasionally, for 1 minute. Transfer to a platter and garnish with the orange slices and sesame seeds.

Serves 6

Oyster Stew

24 small oysters in the shell or bottled
  shucked oysters with their liquor
¼ cup (2 oz/60 g) unsalted butter
1 small yellow onion, minced
1 celery stalk, chopped
pinch of celery seeds, ground in a mortar
  with pestle or in a spice grinder
2 cups (16 fl oz/500 ml) heavy (double)
  cream
2 cups (16 fl oz/500 ml) milk
¼ teaspoon paprika
salt and freshly ground pepper

Quick to prepare, wonderfully rich and delicious, this is a perfect recipe for oyster lovers. Serve the stew with oyster crackers and pour a dry white wine.

*I*f using oysters in the shell, shuck them as directed on page 10, reserving their liquor. Set aside.

In a soup pot over medium heat, melt the butter. Add the onion, celery stalk and celery seeds. Stir well, cover and cook, stirring occasionally, until the vegetables are soft, about 12 minutes.

Add the cream, milk, paprika and salt and pepper to taste and heat just until bubbles form around the edge of the pot. Add the oysters and their liquor and simmer gently until the oysters are cooked, 1–2 minutes; they should be slightly firm to the touch. Do not allow to boil. Ladle into warmed bowls and serve immediately.

Serves 6

Thai Shrimp Salad with Ginger and Mint

½ cup (4 fl oz/125 ml) fish stock or quick fish stock (recipes on pages 12–13) or bottled clam juice

1½ lb (750 g) medium shrimp (prawns), peeled and deveined

4–5 tablespoons (2–2½ fl oz/60–75 ml) fresh lime juice

2 tablespoons fish sauce, optional

1 tablespoon peanut oil

1 teaspoon sugar

1 lemongrass stalk (ends trimmed and tough outer leaves removed), minced, or 1 teaspoon grated lemon zest

1 tablespoon peeled and minced fresh ginger

1 fresh jalapeño or serrano chili pepper, seeded and minced

2 cloves garlic, minced

salt and freshly ground pepper

½ English (hothouse) cucumber, peeled, halved lengthwise and cut crosswise into ¼-inch (6-mm) slices

⅓ cup (1½ oz/45 g) thinly sliced red (Spanish) onion

¼ cup (¼ oz/7 g) fresh mint leaves, cut into thin shreds

4 tablespoons fresh cilantro (fresh coriander) leaves

lime wedges, optional

You can make this zesty salad a day in advance. Serve it on your choice of salad greens as an appetizer or as part of a buffet, or pack it in a cooler for a picnic lunch.

※

*I*n a frying pan, bring the fish stock or clam juice to a boil. Add the shrimp, reduce the heat to low, cover and simmer for 1 minute. Stir lightly, re-cover and cook until the shrimp curl and are firm to the touch, 1 minute longer. Using a slotted spoon, transfer the shrimp to a bowl and let cool slightly. Cover and refrigerate until chilled. Discard the cooking liquid.

In a large bowl, whisk together the lime juice, fish sauce (if using), peanut oil, sugar, lemongrass or lemon zest, ginger, chili pepper, garlic and salt and pepper to taste. Add the chilled shrimp, cucumber, onion, mint and cilantro. Toss well.

Place the salad on a platter. Garnish with lime wedges, if desired, and serve.

Serves 6

Great — Pat Mallory
10-2-00

2 crabs, 1–1½ lb (500–750 g) each,
    cooked
3 tablespoons unsalted butter
1 yellow onion, diced
1 carrot, peeled and diced
2 celery stalks, diced
¼ teaspoon dried tarragon or ½ teaspoon
    chopped fresh tarragon
1½ cups (9 oz/280 g) chopped
    tomatoes (fresh or canned)
1 bay leaf
1 small red bell pepper (capsicum),
    seeded and coarsely chopped
1 cup (8 fl oz/250 ml) dry white wine
3 cups (24 fl oz/750 ml) fish stock or
    quick fish stock *(recipes on pages 12–13)*
    or bottled clam juice
1½ cups (12 fl oz/375 ml) water
¼ cup (2 oz/60 g) white rice
1 cup (8 fl oz/250 ml) heavy (double)
    cream
1 teaspoon fresh lemon juice
salt and freshly ground pepper

Combine w Sherried Crab Bisque
p. 94 – Soups

Creamy Crab Bisque

For an elegant first course, garnish this creamy soup with chopped fresh chives or parsley and serve it with a glass of Champagne.

❋

Clean and crack the crab and remove the meat from the body and legs as directed on page 9; set aside. Remove the meat from each large claw in a single piece, slice and set aside for garnish. Using heavy shears, cut the shells into small pieces; set aside.

In a saucepan over low heat, melt the butter. Add the onion, carrot, celery and tarragon and sauté, stirring, until soft, about 15 minutes. Add the crab shells, tomatoes, bay leaf, bell pepper and wine. Bring to a boil, reduce the heat to low, cover and simmer for 20 minutes. Remove from the heat; let cool slightly.

In a large bowl, combine the fish stock or clam juice and water. Place one-third of the stock mixture and about one-third of the shell mixture in a blender. Pulse a few times until the shells break up. Line a fine-mesh sieve with cheesecloth (muslin) and place over a bowl. Pour the contents of the blender through the sieve. Repeat with the remaining stock and shell mixtures in 2 more batches.

Transfer 2 cups (16 fl oz/500 ml) of the strained mixture to a saucepan and bring to a boil. Add the rice, reduce the heat to low, cover and simmer until very tender, about 20 minutes.

Transfer the rice to a blender, add the remaining strained mixture and blend until very smooth, 1–2 minutes.

Pour the purée into a saucepan and bring to a simmer over low heat. Add the cream, lemon juice and salt and pepper to taste. Strain again through a fine-mesh sieve into a saucepan and bring to a simmer over low heat. Add the reserved crab meat and stir well to heat through. Ladle into bowls and garnish with the reserved claw meat. Serve immediately.

Serves 6–8

Shellfish Gumbo

try

½ cup (4 fl oz/125 ml) vegetable oil
¼ cup (1½ oz/45 g) all-purpose (plain) flour
3 yellow onions, chopped
4 cloves garlic, minced
1 celery stalk, chopped
1 green bell pepper (capsicum), seeded, deribbed and chopped
1 lb (500 g) fresh okra, cut crosswise into slices ½ inch (12 mm) thick, or 3 cups (1 lb/500 g) sliced frozen okra, thawed
1 cup (6 oz/185 g) peeled, halved, seeded and chopped tomatoes (fresh or canned)
4 cups (32 fl oz/1 l) fish stock or quick fish stock (*recipes on pages 12–13*) or bottled clam juice
2 cups (16 fl oz/500 ml) water
¼ teaspoon red pepper flakes
2 bay leaves
1 teaspoon chopped fresh thyme or ½ teaspoon dried thyme
½ lb (250 g) fresh cooked crab meat, picked over to remove shell fragments and cartilage
1 lb (500 g) medium shrimp (prawns), peeled and deveined
½ lb (250 g) bay or sea scallops
6 green (spring) onions, including 2 inches (5 cm) of the tender green tops, thinly sliced
3 tablespoons chopped fresh parsley
salt and freshly ground pepper

Shellfish gumbo is a staple in Louisiana's Cajun country, where there are as many variations as there are cooks. This hearty soup begins with a roux—a cooked mixture of flour and oil— which serves as a thickening agent. Okra adds both a distinctive flavor and extra body. If you like, serve the gumbo spooned over cooked rice and pass a bottle of hot-pepper sauce for your guests to "doctor" their bowls to taste.

❋

In a large soup pot over medium-low heat, warm the vegetable oil. Add the flour and cook, stirring, until the mixture is golden brown, about 10 minutes.

Add the yellow onions, garlic, celery and bell pepper and cook, stirring, until the vegetables wilt, about 10 minutes. Add the okra and tomatoes, cover and simmer gently, stirring occasionally, until thickened slightly, about 10 minutes.

In a bowl or other vessel, combine the fish stock or clam juice and water. Slowly add this mixture to the vegetables, a ladleful at a time, stirring constantly until all of the liquid has been added. Add the red pepper flakes, bay leaves and thyme and simmer gently, uncovered, for 30 minutes.

Add the crab meat, shrimp, scallops, green onions, parsley and salt and pepper to taste. Simmer until the shellfish are cooked and the flavors are blended, about 10 minutes.

Remove the bay leaves and discard. Ladle the gumbo into warmed bowls and serve immediately.

Serves 6

Shrimp Caesar Salad

½ cup (4 fl oz/125 ml) fish stock or quick fish stock (recipes on pages 12–13) or bottled clam juice

1 lb (500 g) medium shrimp (prawns), peeled and deveined

½ French baguette, about 1½ inches (4 cm) in diameter

3 tablespoons plus ¼ cup (2 fl oz/60 ml) pure olive oil

2 cloves garlic

1 teaspoon Dijon mustard

3–4 tablespoons fresh lemon juice

3 anchovy fillets, soaked in cold water to cover for 5 minutes, drained, patted dry and mashed

1 egg yolk

¼ cup (2 fl oz/60 ml) extra-virgin olive oil

salt and freshly ground pepper

2 heads romaine (cos) lettuce, carefully washed and well dried

½ cup (2 oz/60 g) freshly grated Italian Parmesan cheese

Here is a delicious variation on a classic salad. Two types of olive oil are used to balance the fruitiness of the dressing. Marinating the shrimp briefly in the dressing helps to meld the flavors of the salad.

Preheat an oven to 350°F (180°C). Oil a baking sheet.

In a frying pan, bring the fish stock or clam juice to a boil. Add the shrimp, reduce the heat to low, cover and simmer for 1 minute. Uncover, stir lightly, re-cover and cook until the shrimp curl and are firm to the touch, 1 minute longer. Using a slotted spoon, transfer the shrimp to a bowl and let cool slightly. Cover and refrigerate. Reduce the broth over high heat until 2 tablespoons remain. Cover and refrigerate as well.

Cut the baguette into slices ¼ inch (6 mm) thick. Using a pastry brush, brush the slices lightly with the 3 tablespoons pure olive oil. Place in a single layer on the prepared baking sheet and bake, turning occasionally, until golden on both sides, 7–10 minutes. Remove from the oven and rub the top of each crouton with 1 of the garlic cloves. Set aside.

Mince the remaining garlic clove. In a large bowl, whisk together the mustard, lemon juice, anchovies, minced garlic and egg yolk. Combine the ¼ cup (2 fl oz/60 ml) each extra-virgin and pure olive oils and add in a steady stream, whisking constantly. Whisk in the reserved shrimp broth and then add the shrimp, stirring to coat. Let marinate for 10 minutes. Season to taste with salt and pepper. Add the romaine and half of the cheese to the bowl and toss until all of the leaves are evenly coated.

Divide the salad evenly among individual salad plates. Garnish with the croutons and sprinkle with the remaining cheese. Serve immediately.

Serves 6

Fennel, Radish and Scallop Salad with Dill Dressing

½ cup (4 fl oz/125 ml) fish stock or
   quick fish stock (recipes on pages 12–13)
   or bottled clam juice
1½ lb (750 g) sea scallops, cut
   horizontally into slices ¼ inch
   (6 mm) thick
2 fennel bulbs, preferably with feathery
   tops intact
3–5 tablespoons (2–2½ fl oz/60–75 ml)
   fresh lemon juice
6 tablespoons (3 fl oz/90 ml) extra-
   virgin olive oil
1 clove garlic, minced
3 tablespoons chopped fresh dill
salt and freshly ground pepper
1 bunch radishes, trimmed and thinly
   sliced

This salad has a crisp texture, attractive presentation of colors and refreshingly light flavors. Enjoy it as a first course or as a light main course. If you like, garnish with fresh dill sprigs or lemon slices.

*In a frying pan, bring the fish stock or clam juice to a boil. Add the scallops, reduce the heat to medium, cover and simmer for 1 minute. Turn the scallops over and continue simmering until almost firm to the touch, about 1 minute longer. Using a slotted spoon, transfer the scallops to a large bowl. Cover and refrigerate. Discard the cooking liquid.

Cut off the feathery tops from the fennel bulbs and set aside. Remove the stalks and any tough or bruised outer leaves from the bulbs and discard. Using a sharp knife, cut each bulb in half lengthwise. Then slice the bulb halves crosswise into paper-thin slices. Place the slices in a large bowl, add 1 tablespoon of the lemon juice and toss well. Cover and refrigerate. Chop 1 tablespoon of the fennel tops and reserve; discard the remaining fennel tops.

In a small bowl, whisk together the olive oil, 2 table-spoons of the lemon juice, the garlic, fennel tops and the dill. Season to taste with salt and pepper. Taste and adjust seasoning with more lemon juice, if needed.

Add the sliced fennel and the radishes to the scallops. Add the dressing and toss gently to mix well. Transfer to a platter and let stand for 10 minutes at room temperature before serving.

Serves 6

Lobster and Corn Chowder

7 cups (56 fl oz/1.75 l) water or court bouillon (*recipe on page 13*)

salt

2 live lobsters, about 1¼ lb (625 g) each

½ cup (4 fl oz/125 ml) dry white wine

½ lb (250 g) potatoes, peeled and cut into ½-inch (12-mm) dice

6 small ears of corn, husks and silks removed

1 tablespoon unsalted butter

1 yellow onion, finely chopped

½ cup (4 fl oz/125 ml) heavy (double) cream

freshly ground pepper

1 tablespoon coarsely chopped fresh parsley or 6 parsley sprigs

Two live crabs can be substituted for the lobster, but cook them for 12 minutes. Clean and crack the crabs and remove the meat from the shells as directed on page 9, then use the shells for the broth.

*In a stockpot, bring the water or court bouillon to a boil. If using water, add 1 tablespoon salt once it boils. Add the lobsters and cook until the shells are red, about 7 minutes. Using tongs, lift out the lobsters and let cool. Reserve the lobster broth.

Remove the lobster meat from the shells as directed on page 8. Dice the meat into ½-inch (12-mm) pieces and set aside. Reserve the shells but discard the tomalley, black intestinal vein and any other organs. Cut the head section into small pieces and add them, along with all the shells and the wine, to the reserved lobster broth. Simmer over medium heat, uncovered, for 20 minutes. Strain through a fine-mesh sieve lined with cheesecloth (muslin) and reserve.

Meanwhile, fill a saucepan three-fourths full of water and bring to a boil. Add salt to taste and the potatoes and boil until tender, about 10 minutes. Drain and set aside.

Using a sharp knife, cut the kernels from the ears of corn. You should have 2–2½ cups (12–15 oz/375–470 g). Set aside.

Rinse the stockpot, place over medium heat and melt the butter. Add the onion and sauté, stirring, until soft, about 10 minutes. Set aside 1 cup (6 oz/185 g) of the corn kernels. Add the remaining corn to the pot along with the lobster broth. Simmer uncovered for 20 minutes, then purée in a blender until smooth. Press through a fine-mesh sieve into a clean saucepan.

Place the pan over medium heat. Add the cream, lobster meat and reserved corn and potatoes. Season to taste with salt and pepper. Simmer for 5 minutes to heat through; do not boil. Ladle into warmed bowls and garnish with the parsley.

Serves 6

Oysters on the Half Shell with Shallot-Pepper Sauce

½ cup (4 fl oz/125 ml) dry white wine

¼ cup (2 fl oz/60 ml) Champagne
   vinegar or white wine vinegar, or
   to taste

4 shallots, minced

coarsely ground pepper

crushed or shaved ice

36 oysters in the shell, well scrubbed

lemon wedges, optional

fresh parsley sprigs, optional

The French name for the sauce that accompanies these raw oysters is mignonette. For a more American-style dish, omit the shallot sauce and make a traditional cocktail sauce by seasoning ketchup with prepared horseradish, hot-pepper sauce and fresh lemon juice to taste. Paired with well-buttered rye bread, the oysters are a light and refreshing first course. Serve them on crushed ice on a single large platter or on individual plates.

❦

In a small bowl, stir together the wine, vinegar, shallots and pepper to taste. Taste and adjust the seasoning with additional vinegar.

Place the bowl of shallot-pepper sauce in the center of a large platter. Surround the bowl with a bed of crushed or shaved ice.

Shuck the oysters as directed on page 10, discarding the top shells and detaching the oysters from their bottom shells. Be sure not to spill the liquor from the bottom shells. Nest the oysters in their shells on the ice.

Garnish with lemon wedges and parsley sprigs, if desired. Serve immediately.

Serves 6

Crab Fritters with Red Pepper Mayonnaise

1 cup (5 oz/155 g) all-purpose (plain) flour
½ teaspoon salt
2 egg yolks
2 tablespoons olive oil
¾ cup (6 fl oz/180 ml) beer, at room temperature

FOR THE RED PEPPER MAYONNAISE:
1 red bell pepper (capsicum)
1 cup (8 fl oz/250 ml) mayonnaise, store-bought or homemade (recipe on page 13)
3 tablespoons chopped fresh chives
pinch of cayenne pepper
2 cloves garlic, minced
2 tablespoons fresh lemon juice
salt and freshly ground pepper

corn oil or peanut oil for deep-frying
2 egg whites
¾ lb (375 g) fresh cooked crab meat, picked over for shell fragments and cartilage
lemon wedges, optional
fresh parsley sprigs, optional

Try serving these fritters with rémoulade (recipe on page 64), an herb vinaigrette or fresh tomato salsa in place of the mayonnaise.

❧

*P*reheat a broiler (griller).

In a large bowl, sift together the flour and salt. Make a well in the center and add the egg yolks, olive oil and beer; whisk to mix well. Let the batter rest for 1 hour at room temperature.

To make the mayonnaise, cut the bell pepper in half lengthwise and remove the stem, seeds and ribs. Place cut side down on a baking sheet. Broil (grill) until blackened, 6–10 minutes. Transfer the pepper to a plastic or paper bag, close tightly and let cool for 10 minutes. Using your fingers, peel off the skin; chop the pepper coarsely and place in a blender or in a mortar. Blend or crush with a pestle until smooth. Place the mayonnaise in a small bowl and stir in the pepper purée, chives, cayenne, garlic, lemon juice and salt and ground pepper to taste. Cover and refrigerate until serving.

In a deep saucepan, pour in oil to a depth of 2 inches (5 cm). Heat to 375°F (190°C) on a deep-frying thermometer, or until a little batter sizzles on contact. Meanwhile, in a bowl, beat the egg whites until stiff. Gently fold the egg whites and crab meat into the batter.

Drop the crab mixture by heaping tablespoonfuls into the hot oil; do not crowd the pan. Fry, turning often, until golden brown, about 2 minutes. Using a slotted spoon, transfer to paper towels to drain.

Arrange the hot fritters on a platter. If desired, garnish with lemon and parsley. Serve the mayonnaise on the side.

Serves 6

Shrimp Quesadillas with Avocado-Tomatillo Salsa

try

FOR THE SALSA:

1 lb (500 g) tomatillos, husks removed

5 tablespoons (¼ oz/7 g) chopped fresh cilantro (fresh coriander)

¼ cup (1½ oz/45 g) minced red (Spanish) onion

2–3 tablespoons fresh lime juice

1 tablespoon extra-virgin olive oil

½ fresh jalapeño or serrano chili pepper, seeded and minced

1 avocado, halved, pitted, peeled and cut into ½-inch (12-mm) cubes

salt and freshly ground pepper

FOR THE QUESADILLAS:

½ cup (4 fl oz/125 ml) fish stock or quick fish stock (*recipes on pages 12–13*) or bottled clam juice

1 lb (500 g) medium shrimp (prawns), peeled and deveined

1 cup (4 oz/125 g) coarsely grated Monterey Jack cheese

1 cup (4 oz/125 g) coarsely grated mozzarella cheese

1 cup (4 oz/125 g) coarsely grated white Cheddar cheese

4 green (spring) onions, including 2 inches (5 cm) of the tender green tops, thinly sliced

6 large flour tortillas

The quesadillas can also be filled with cooked crab meat or scallops. If fresh tomatillos are unavailable, use canned (drained) ones.

❧

To make the salsa, fill a saucepan three-fourths full of water and bring to a boil. Immerse the tomatillos in the boiling water for 20 seconds. Drain and let cool. (Omit this step if using canned tomatillos.)

Place the cooled tomatillos in a food processor or a blender. Pulse a few times until almost smooth but some chunks still remain. Transfer the tomatillos to a bowl. Add the cilantro, red onion, lime juice, olive oil, jalapeño or serrano chili pepper, avocado and salt and pepper to taste. Stir well; you should have about 2½ cups (20 fl oz/625 ml). Set aside.

To make the quesadillas, in a frying pan, bring the fish stock or clam juice to a boil. Add the shrimp, reduce the heat to low, cover and simmer until the shrimp curl and are almost firm to the touch, about 1 minute. Using a slotted spoon, transfer the shrimp to a cutting board; chop coarsely.

In a bowl, combine the shrimp, the 3 cheeses and green onions and stir to mix. Distribute the mixture evenly among 3 of the tortillas. Top with the remaining tortillas to form the quesadillas.

Place a large frying pan over medium heat. When it is hot, slip 1 quesadilla into the pan and cook until the cheese begins to melt, 2–3 minutes. Turn the quesadilla over and continue to cook on the other side until the cheese is melted and the tortilla is slightly golden, 1–2 minutes. Remove from the pan and keep warm. Repeat with the remaining quesadillas.

Cut each quesadilla into 6 wedges and serve immediately with the salsa.

Serves 6

Baked Mussels with Feta Cheese and Tomatoes

¼ cup (2 fl oz/60 ml) olive oil
½ yellow onion, finely chopped
2 cups (12 oz/375 g) peeled, halved,
  seeded and coarsely chopped
  tomatoes (fresh or canned)
1 cup (8 fl oz/250 ml) dry white wine
¼ teaspoon dried oregano
pinch of red pepper flakes
1 teaspoon red wine vinegar
2 lb (1 kg) mussels, debearded and
  well scrubbed
6 oz (185 g) feta cheese, crumbled
salt and freshly ground pepper
1 tablespoon coarsely chopped fresh
  parsley

Feta, a mildly salty, moist white cheese, is made from sheep's or goat's milk. The combination of shellfish and feta is eaten all over Greece, prepared with shrimp as well as mussels.

🐚

*I*n a large frying pan over low heat, warm the olive oil. Add the onion and sauté, stirring, until soft, about 10 minutes. Increase the heat to high. Add the tomatoes, wine, oregano, red pepper flakes and vinegar and stir well. Reduce the heat to medium-low and simmer uncovered, stirring occasionally, until thick, about 20 minutes.

Meanwhile, preheat an oven to 400°F (200°C).

Discard any mussels that do not close to the touch. Add the mussels to the frying pan. Cover and cook over medium heat, shaking the pan periodically, until all the mussels open, 2–4 minutes. Using a slotted spoon, transfer the mussels from the pan to a plate. Discard any unopened mussels. Remove the mussels from their shells and discard the shells. Place the mussels in a 1-qt (1-l) baking dish. Add the tomato sauce, feta and salt and pepper to taste. Stir gently.

Bake until the tomato sauce bubbles around the edge, 10–15 minutes. Remove from the oven and garnish with the parsley. Serve immediately.

Serves 6

Sizzling Scallops

1 lb (500 g) sea or bay scallops
3 tablespoons unsalted butter
¼ cup (1½ oz/45 g) minced yellow
  onion
1 cup (3 oz/90 g) thinly sliced fresh
  mushrooms
½ cup (4 fl oz/125 ml) dry white wine
1 cup (8 fl oz/250 ml) heavy (double)
  cream
2–3 teaspoons fresh lemon juice
½ cup (2 oz/60 g) freshly grated
  Parmesan cheese
salt and freshly ground pepper
1 tablespoon chopped fresh parsley

This variation on the classic French coquilles St. Jacques uses a reduced cream sauce instead of the traditional flour-thickened béchamel. You will need 6 flameproof scallop shells or scallop-shaped serving dishes for baking the scallop-and-mushroom mixture. Look for them at a specialty cookware shop. Small (¾ cup/6 fl oz/180 ml) ramekins can also be used. Be sure to accompany the dish with plenty of bread for sopping up the delectable cream sauce.

*I*f using sea scallops, cut them horizontally into slices ¼ inch (6 mm) thick. If using bay scallops, leave them whole.

Preheat a broiler (griller).

In a frying pan over medium heat, melt 1 tablespoon of the butter. Add the scallops and sauté until just firm to the touch, about 2 minutes. Using a slotted spoon, transfer the scallops to a plate. Set aside.

Add the remaining 2 tablespoons butter to the same pan over medium heat. Add the onion and sauté, stirring, until soft, about 5 minutes. Raise the heat to high, add the mushrooms and sauté, stirring occasionally, until the liquid evaporates, about 5 minutes. Add the white wine and cook until reduced by half. Reduce the heat to medium-low, add the cream and simmer until thickened, 2–3 minutes. Add the lemon juice, Parmesan cheese, scallops and salt and pepper to taste and stir to combine.

Divide the hot scallop mixture among 6 flameproof scallop shells arranged in a shallow pan. Slip under the broiler and broil (grill) until the tops are golden and bubbling at the edges, 1–2 minutes.

Sprinkle with the parsley and serve immediately.

Serves 6

Spanish Clams with Tomatoes and Herbs

Good !,

9-2-12

4 tablespoons (2 fl oz/60 ml) olive oil
1 yellow onion, chopped
¾ cup (4½ oz/140 g) peeled, halved,
    seeded and chopped tomatoes
    (fresh or canned)
1 tablespoon tomato paste
½ cup (4 fl oz/125 ml) dry white wine
1 cup (8 fl oz/250 ml) fish stock or
    quick fish stock (*recipes on pages 12–13*)
    or bottled clam juice
salt and freshly ground pepper
2 lb (1 kg) clams, well scrubbed
1 large clove garlic, minced
2 tablespoons chopped fresh parsley

Spanish cooks have paired clams with fresh tomatoes for centuries. Mussels can be substituted for the clams; be sure to remove their beards and scrub the shells well before adding them to the pan.

In a frying pan over medium heat, warm 2 tablespoons of the olive oil. Add the onion and sauté, stirring, until it begins to turn golden, 12–15 minutes. Add the tomatoes and tomato paste and continue to sauté, stirring occasionally, until thickened, 5–6 minutes. Add the wine and cook uncovered over medium heat until reduced by half, about 5 minutes. Add the fish stock or clam juice, raise the heat to high and cook uncovered until thickened, about 5 minutes. Remove from the heat and let cool slightly.

In a food processor fitted with the metal blade or in a blender, purée the tomato mixture until smooth. Season to taste with salt and pepper. Set aside.

In a frying pan large enough to hold the clams in a single layer, warm the remaining 2 tablespoons olive oil over high heat. Discard any clams that do not close to the touch. Add the garlic, parsley and clams, cover and cook, shaking the pan periodically, until the clams open, 3–5 minutes depending upon the size. Discard any unopened clams.

Using a slotted spoon, transfer the clams to a plate and keep warm. Add the puréed tomato mixture to the same pan and boil uncovered until reduced by one-fourth. Add the clams and mix well.

Transfer to a platter and serve immediately.

Serves 6

Parchment-Baked Oysters with Saffron-Orange Butter

24 medium oysters in the shell or
   drained bottled shucked oysters
1 red bell pepper (capsicum)
½ cup (2 oz/60 g) diced red (Spanish)
   onion (¼-inch/6-mm dice)
10 large radishes, thinly sliced
4 tablespoons finely chopped fresh
   chives
4 tablespoons chopped fresh parsley
salt and freshly ground pepper
1 teaspoon fresh orange juice
½ teaspoon grated orange zest
¼ teaspoon saffron threads, steeped in
   1 teaspoon hot water
¼ cup (2 oz/60 g) unsalted butter, at
   room temperature, plus 2 tablespoons
   unsalted butter, melted

Cut into these parchment packets in the kitchen, or place them on individual plates for guests to open themselves.

❧

*I*f using oysters in the shell, shuck them as directed on page 10. Set aside. Preheat a broiler (griller).

Cut the bell pepper in half lengthwise and remove the stem, seeds and ribs. Place cut side down on a baking sheet. Broil (grill) until blackened, 6–10 minutes. Transfer to a plastic or paper bag, close tightly and let cool for 10 minutes. Using your fingers, peel off the skin; cut the pepper into ¼-inch (6-mm) dice. Set aside.

Meanwhile, in a small bowl, combine the onion with water to cover. Let stand for 5 minutes, then drain.

In a bowl, combine the onion, roasted pepper, radishes, chives, parsley and salt and pepper to taste. Set aside. In another small bowl, mash together the orange juice and zest, saffron and water, the ¼ cup (2 oz/60 g) butter and salt and pepper to taste. Preheat an oven to 400°F (200°C).

Cut out 6 hearts from parchment paper, each 12 inches (30 cm) tall and 12 inches (30 cm) wide at its widest point. Brush the hearts on one side only with the melted butter. Place 4 oysters on the right side of each heart. Top the oysters with equal amounts of the vegetable mixture. Season with salt and pepper. Dot each portion with the saffron-orange butter. Fold the other half of each heart over the filling and crease the edges together securely so the juices will not escape. Place on baking sheets.

Bake the packets until they have puffed considerably, 6–10 minutes. Remove from the oven and cut open the top of each packet. Serve immediately.

Serves 6

Pizza with Shrimp and Aioli

2 unbaked ready-made 9-inch (23-cm) pizza crusts or ¾ lb (375 g) purchased pizza dough

FOR THE AIOLI:
⅓ cup (3 fl oz/80 ml) mayonnaise, store-bought or homemade (recipe on page 13)
1 clove garlic, minced
2–3 teaspoons warm water

FOR THE TOPPING:
¼ lb (125 g) Fontina cheese, coarsely grated
¼ lb (125 g) mozzarella cheese, coarsely grated
2 tablespoons olive oil
½ small red (Spanish) onion, thinly sliced
½ teaspoon red pepper flakes
6 oz (185 g) small shrimp (prawns), peeled and deveined
2 teaspoons chopped fresh parsley

Using a pizza stone (or unglazed terra-cotta tiles) results in a particularly crispy crust. If you do not have a pizza stone, bake the pizzas on a baking sheet or pizza pan. Feel free to substitute a favorite pizza dough for the purchased crusts or dough.

❧

Place a pizza stone on the lowest rack of an oven and preheat the oven to 500°F (260°C).

Place a pizza crust on a well-floured pizza peel (wide wooden bakers' paddle) or a rimless baking sheet. If using the pizza dough, divide the dough in half and, on a floured work surface, roll out one half into a 9-inch (23-cm) round, then transfer it to a peel.

To make the aioli, in a small bowl, stir together the mayonnaise and garlic. Add enough of the warm water to make the mixture barely fluid. Set aside.

To make the topping, in another small bowl, combine the Fontina and mozzarella. Brush 1 tablespoon of the olive oil on the dough round to within ½ inch (12 mm) of the edge. Sprinkle half of the cheese over the oil. Spread half of the onion over the cheese; then sprinkle with the red pepper flakes.

Slide the pizza directly onto the pizza stone and bake for 5 minutes. Using the peel (or a baking sheet), remove from the oven and arrange half of the shrimp on top. Slide the pizza back onto the stone and continue to bake until the shrimp are cooked and the dough is crisp and golden, 4–5 minutes longer.

Using the peel (or a baking sheet), remove the pizza from the oven. Drizzle with half of the aioli and sprinkle with half of the parsley. Cut into wedges and serve immediately. Repeat with the remaining ingredients to make a second pizza.

Makes two 9-inch (23-cm) pizzas; serves 6

Broiled Oysters with Herbed Bread Crumbs

36 oysters in the shell, well scrubbed

6 tablespoons (3 oz/90 g) unsalted butter

4 large shallots, minced

1 clove garlic, minced

2½ cups (5 oz/155 g) fresh bread crumbs

2 tablespoons chopped fresh parsley

1 tablespoon chopped fresh chives

½ teaspoon chopped fresh oregano, plus oregano sprigs for garnish

½ teaspoon chopped fresh thyme, plus thyme sprigs for garnish

2 tablespoons fish stock or quick fish stock *(recipes on pages 12–13)* or bottled clam juice

2–3 teaspoons fresh lemon juice

salt and freshly ground pepper

lemon wedges

This is a popular dish wherever fresh oysters are found. The stuffing can also be varied with the addition of 3 tablespoons chopped wilted spinach, green (spring) onions, fennel bulb or fresh mushrooms.

❧

Shuck the oysters as directed on page 10, reserving their liquor in a bowl. Discard the top shells and detach the oysters from the bottom shells. Place the opened oysters on their bottom shells on a baking sheet. Cover and refrigerate the oysters and their liquor.

Preheat an oven to 450°F (230°C).

In a frying pan over medium heat, melt 4 tablespoons (2 oz/60 g) of the butter. Add the shallots and sauté, stirring, until soft, about 8 minutes. Add the garlic and continue to sauté for 1 minute. Add the bread crumbs, parsley, chives and chopped oregano and thyme; sauté, stirring occasionally, until the bread crumbs are lightly golden, about 10 minutes. Add the reserved oyster liquor, the fish stock or clam juice, lemon juice and salt and pepper to taste. Mix well and remove from the heat. The stuffing should be slightly moist.

Spoon the stuffing atop the oysters, dividing it evenly. In a small saucepan or frying pan, melt the remaining 2 tablespoons butter. Drizzle the butter evenly over the stuffing.

Bake the oysters until very hot, about 6 minutes. Remove from the oven.

Preheat a broiler (griller). Broil (grill) the oysters until the stuffing is a light golden brown, 1–2 minutes.

Garnish with lemon wedges and the oregano and thyme sprigs. Serve hot.

Serves 6

Scallop Ceviche with Sweet and Hot Peppers

1 lb (500 g) sea or bay scallops
¾ cup (6 fl oz/180 ml) fresh lime juice
½ green bell pepper (capsicum)
½ red bell pepper (capsicum)
½ yellow bell pepper (capsicum)
¼ cup (2 fl oz/60 ml) extra-virgin
   olive oil
2 cloves garlic, minced
½ cup (¾ oz/20 g) coarsely chopped
   fresh cilantro (fresh coriander)
2 fresh jalapeño chili peppers, seeded
   and minced
2 small tomatoes, cut into ¼-inch
   (6-mm) dice
¼ cup (1 oz/30 g) diced red (Spanish)
   onion (¼-inch/6-mm dice)
salt and freshly ground pepper
lime wedges

Ceviche is a dish of Latin American origin in which raw scallops or other seafood are "cooked" in citrus juice. The juice causes the fish to firm up and become opaque much in the same way that heat does. Cod or snapper fillets, cut into 1-inch (2.5-cm) chunks, can be substituted for the scallops. And try using avocado slices as a garnish in addition to the lime wedges. Serve with crisp tortilla chips.

If you are using sea scallops, cut them horizontally into slices ¼ inch (6 mm) thick. If you are using bay scallops, leave them whole. Place the scallops in a bowl, add the lime juice and toss to mix. Cover and refrigerate for 1 hour.

   Remove the stems, seeds and ribs from the bell pepper halves. Cut into strips 1 inch (2.5 cm) long and ⅛ inch (3 mm) wide.

   Add to the scallops the olive oil, garlic, cilantro, chili peppers, bell pepper strips, tomatoes, onion and salt and pepper to taste. Mix well. Garnish with lime wedges and serve immediately.

Serves 6

Panfried Croutons Topped with Spiced Crab

1 clove garlic
⅓ cup (3 fl oz/80 ml) mayonnaise, store-bought or homemade (recipe on page 13)
1 teaspoon fresh lemon juice
⅛–¼ teaspoon cayenne pepper
½ teaspoon sweet paprika
4 tablespoons finely chopped fresh chives
3 green (spring) onions, including 2 inches (5 cm) of the tender green tops, thinly sliced
salt and freshly ground pepper
6 oz (185 g) fresh cooked crab meat, picked over for shell fragments and cartilage
3 tablespoons unsalted butter
3 tablespoons olive oil
½ French baguette, cut on a sharp diagonal into slices ¼ inch (6 mm) thick
lemon wedges

These croutons are also delicious as an accompaniment to a bowl of vegetable soup or alongside a garden salad. The chunky topping can be made with other shellfish such as cooked and chopped shrimp (prawns), lobster or scallops.

Crush the garlic with a pestle in a mortar (or pass it through a garlic press) to form a smooth paste. Transfer to a small bowl. Add the mayonnaise, lemon juice, cayenne, paprika, chives, green onions and salt and pepper to taste. Mix well. Add the crab meat and stir to combine.

In a large frying pan over medium heat, melt 1 tablespoon of the butter with 1 tablespoon of the olive oil. Place about one-third of the bread in a single layer in the pan and sauté, turning once, until the bread is golden on both sides, 2–3 minutes. Using a slotted spatula, transfer the bread slices to a plate. Repeat with the remaining butter, oil and bread slices in two more batches.

Spread the spiced crab mixture on the panfried bread slices, dividing it equally among them. Arrange on a platter and garnish with lemon wedges. Serve immediately.

Serves 6

Try 1-14-03

Good!

Crab Cakes with Rémoulade Sauce

FOR THE RÉMOULADE SAUCE:
1 cup (8 fl oz/250 ml) mayonnaise
3 tablespoons Dijon mustard
2–3 tablespoons white wine vinegar
1 tablespoon paprika
2 tablespoons grated prepared horseradish
1 clove garlic, finely chopped
⅓ cup (1 oz/30 g) finely chopped green (spring) onions
⅓ cup (2 oz/60 g) finely chopped celery
2 tablespoons finely chopped fresh parsley
2 tablespoons tomato sauce or ketchup
salt and freshly ground pepper

FOR THE CRAB CAKES:
2 tablespoons unsalted butter
6 green (spring) onions, including 2 inches (5 cm) of the tender green tops, thinly sliced
¾ cup (4 oz/125 g) chopped celery *green pepper*
1 cup (4 oz/125 g) finely crushed saltine crackers
1 tablespoon dry mustard
1 teaspoon hot-pepper sauce, such as Tabasco
2 teaspoons Worcestershire sauce
2 eggs, well beaten
¼ cup (2 fl oz/60 ml) mayonnaise
3 tablespoons finely chopped fresh parsley
1 lb (500 g) fresh cooked crab meat, picked over for shell fragments and cartilage
salt and freshly ground pepper
about 2 cups (4 oz/125 g) fresh bread crumbs
4 tablespoons (2 fl oz/60 ml) vegetable oil or unsalted butter

1 Crab = 2 crabcakes

You can also serve these crab cakes with red pepper mayonnaise (recipe on page 44) or aioli (page 56). Garnish with lemon or lime wedges and the leafy tops of celery stalks.

To make the rémoulade, in a bowl, stir together all the ingredients, including salt and pepper to taste. Mix well. You should have about 2 cups (16 fl oz/500 ml). Cover and refrigerate until serving.

To make the crab cakes, in a large frying pan over low heat, melt the 2 tablespoons butter. Add the green onions and celery, cover and cook, stirring occasionally, until soft, about 10 minutes. Using a slotted spoon, transfer the onions and celery to a bowl and let cool. Discard the butter.

To the cooled onion-celery mixture, add the crushed saltines, mustard, hot-pepper sauce, Worcestershire sauce, eggs, mayonnaise, parsley, crab meat and salt and pepper to taste. Mix well. If the mixture seems too wet to hold its shape, add enough of the bread crumbs (about ½ cup/1 oz/30 g) as needed to absorb the moisture. Shape the mixture into six cakes, each 3 inches (7.5 cm) in diameter and ½ inch (12 mm) thick. Place the remaining crumbs in a shallow bowl. Dredge the cakes lightly in the crumbs.

In a frying pan over medium heat, warm 2 tablespoons of the vegetable oil or melt 2 tablespoons of the butter. Add half of the crab cakes and sauté, turning once, until golden brown, about 3 minutes on each side. Using a slotted spatula, transfer to paper towels to drain. Keep warm. Sauté the remaining crab cakes in the same way, using the remaining oil or butter.

Serve the crab cakes immediately with the rémoulade sauce.

Serves 6

Baked Filo Triangles with Moroccan-Spiced Shellfish

2 tablespoons olive oil
¼ lb (125 g) bay scallops
¼ lb (125 g) medium shrimp (prawns),
 peeled and deveined
2 cloves garlic, minced
¼ cup (1½ oz/45 g) finely chopped
 yellow onion
1 large tomato, chopped
4 tablespoons chopped fresh cilantro
 (fresh coriander)
¾ teaspoon ground cumin
pinch of cayenne pepper
pinch of saffron threads, crumbled
¼ cup (½ oz/15 g) fresh bread crumbs
salt and freshly ground pepper
½ lb (250 g) filo sheets
½ cup (4 oz/125 g) unsalted butter,
 melted

Just before serving, squeeze a fresh lemon wedge over the tops of these feather-light triangles for a refreshing hint of citrus.

In a frying pan over low heat, warm 1 tablespoon of the oil. Add the scallops, shrimp and half of the garlic and sauté, stirring, until the shellfish are almost firm to the touch, about 2 minutes. Transfer to a cutting board and chop coarsely. Set aside.

Add the remaining 1 tablespoon oil to the same pan and place over medium heat. Add the onion and tomato and sauté, stirring occasionally, until the onion is tender, about 10 minutes. Add the remaining garlic, the cilantro, cumin, cayenne and saffron. Simmer gently until the moisture evaporates, about 10 minutes. Remove from the heat and mix in the shellfish mixture and bread crumbs. Season to taste with salt and ground pepper.

Preheat an oven to 375°F (190°C). Cut the stack of filo sheets lengthwise into strips about 3 inches (7.5 cm) wide. Working with one at a time and keeping the remaining strips covered with a damp cloth, brush lightly with melted butter. Top with a second strip and brush it lightly with butter. Place a teaspoonful of the shellfish mixture near one end. Fold the end over the filling on the diagonal to form a triangle, so the bottom edge of the strip now touches the left side of it. Bring the bottom point of the triangle up to align with the straight edge, and continue folding until you reach the top of the strip. Brush the triangle lightly with butter and place, fold side down, on a greased baking sheet. Repeat with the remaining strips and filling.

Bake until golden, about 15 minutes. Transfer to a platter and serve immediately.

Makes about 30 triangles; serves 6

...... (.... g) .... scallops
2 tablespoons olive oil
grated zest of 1 lemon
freshly ground pepper
4 large, long red bell peppers
   (capsicums)

FOR THE VINAIGRETTE:
2 tablespoons red wine vinegar
6 tablespoons (3 fl oz/90 ml) extra-
   virgin olive oil
1 tablespoon chopped fresh parsley
½ teaspoon chopped fresh oregano,
   optional
salt

Yellow bell peppers can be substituted for the red peppers. Grill your favorite vegetables to serve alongside the scallops. If you like, drizzle the brochettes with a good-quality pesto sauce in place of the vinaigrette.

❋

Soak 12 bamboo skewers in water to cover for 30 minutes. Meanwhile, in a bowl, combine the scallops, olive oil, lemon zest and ground pepper to taste. Set aside. Preheat a broiler (griller).

Cut the peppers in half lengthwise and remove the stems, seeds and ribs. Place cut side down on a baking sheet. Broil (grill) until blackened, 6–10 minutes. Transfer to a plastic or paper bag, close tightly and let cool for 10 minutes. Using your fingers or a small knife, peel off the skin. Cut the peppers lengthwise into strips ¾ inch (2 cm) wide.

Prepare a fire in a charcoal grill, or leave the broiler preheated. Drain the skewers. Wrap a pepper strip around a scallop to cover completely, overlapping the pepper ends. Secure the strip in place by running a skewer through the scallop and pepper. Repeat with the remaining pepper strips and scallops, dividing the wrapped scallops evenly among the skewers.

To make the vinaigrette, in a small bowl, whisk together the vinegar, olive oil, parsley, oregano and salt and pepper to taste.

Place the skewers on a grill rack over a medium-hot fire and grill, turning once, until the scallops are almost firm to the touch, 1–2 minutes on each side. Alternatively, place on a broiling pan and broil (grill), turning once, until almost firm to the touch, about 3 minutes per side. Transfer the skewers to a platter and drizzle with the dressing. Serve immediately.

Serves 6

Fried Oyster BLTs

24 oysters in the shell or drained
   bottled shucked oysters

2 eggs

2 tablespoons milk

salt and freshly ground pepper

½ cup (2½ oz/75 g) all-purpose (plain)
   flour

2 cups (8 oz/250 g) fine saltine cracker
   crumbs

corn, peanut or vegetable oil for
   deep-frying

½ lb (250 g) sliced bacon

12 slices sourdough, multigrain or
   white bread

⅓ cup (3 fl oz/80 ml) mayonnaise,
   store-bought or homemade
   (*recipe on page 13*)

1 small head lettuce, leaves separated

2 large ripe tomatoes, thinly sliced

Tucking fried oysters into this traditional American sandwich gives it a welcome seafood accent. Sliced avocado or Swiss cheese are also good additions. And for some added zip, mix a little minced garlic into the mayonnaise.

❋

*I*f using oysters in the shell, shuck them as directed on page 10.

In a small bowl, lightly beat the eggs until blended, then beat in the milk and salt and pepper to taste. Place the flour and salt and pepper to taste in another small bowl, and the cracker crumbs and salt and pepper to taste in a third bowl. Dip the oysters in the egg mixture, then in the flour, then in the egg again and lastly, in the cracker crumbs. Place on a baking sheet until ready to cook.

In a deep saucepan, pour in oil to a depth of 2 inches (5 cm). Heat to 375°F (190°C) on a deep-frying thermometer, or until the oil ripples and a bead of batter sizzles on contact.

While the oil is heating, in a frying pan over medium heat, fry the bacon in a single layer until crisp, 4–5 minutes. Transfer to paper towels to drain.

At the same time, toast the bread until golden in a preheated broiler (griller), toaster or toaster oven.

When the oil is ready, slip the oysters into the pan, a few at a time, and fry until golden, 1½–2 minutes. Using a slotted spoon, transfer to paper towels to drain briefly.

Spread each piece of toast on one side with the mayonnaise. Top 6 slices of the toast with the lettuce, bacon, tomatoes and oysters. Place the remaining 6 slices of toast on top. Cut the sandwiches in half and serve immediately.

Serves 6

salt and freshly ground pepper
3 lb (1.5 kg) mixed live lobster(s) and
   fresh cooked crab(s)
2 lb (1 kg) mixed clams and mussels,
   well scrubbed and mussels debearded
½ cup (4 fl oz/125 ml) dry white wine
⅓ cup (3 fl oz/80 ml) white wine
   vinegar
3 shallots, finely chopped
6 fresh parsley stems
pinch of fresh or dried thyme
1 bay leaf
1 cup (8 oz/250 g) unsalted butter,
   at room temperature, cut into
   1-tablespoon pieces
1–2 teaspoons fresh lemon juice
1–2 teaspoons fresh lime juice
lemon and/or lime wedges

Add salt to taste and the lobster(s) and boil until dark red and fully cooked, about 10 minutes. Using tongs, transfer to a plate to cool. Bring the crab(s) to room temperature. Discard any clams and mussels that do not close to the touch, and place the others in a bowl with the remaining 2 tablespoons oil, tossing to coat evenly. Set aside. Prepare a fire in a charcoal grill.

Thirty minutes before serving, in a saucepan over high heat, combine the wine, vinegar, shallots, parsley stems, thyme and bay leaf. Boil until reduced to 3 tablespoons. Let cool slightly, then reduce the heat to low. Add the butter, 1 tablespoon at a time, whisking vigorously until incorporated. When all of the butter has been added, strain the mixture through a fine-mesh sieve. Season to taste with salt, pepper and the lemon and lime juices. Place in the top pan of a double boiler or in a heatproof bowl placed over (but not touching) warm water.

Place the lobster(s) and crab(s) on the grill rack and grill, turning once, until hot, 4–5 minutes. Transfer to a platter. Place the clams and mussels on the grill rack, sprinkle with salt, cover and cook until they open, about 4 minutes. Discard any unopened ones. Squeeze 2–4 lemon and/or lime wedges over them and transfer to the platter. Place the scallops and shrimp on the grill rack and grill, turning once, until firm to the touch, about 3 minutes. Add to the platter. Just before serving, clean and crack the lobster(s) and crab(s) as directed on pages 8–9. Serve the shellfish immediately with the lemon-lime butter.

Serves 6

Shrimp, Green Bean and Ginger Stir-Fry

1½ lb (750 g) large shrimp (prawns),
   peeled and deveined

3 cloves garlic, minced

¼–½ teaspoon cayenne pepper

3 tablespoons peeled and minced fresh
   ginger

1 tablespoon rice wine vinegar

2 teaspoons Asian sesame oil

1 lb (500 g) young green beans or
   Chinese long beans, trimmed and
   cut into 1½-inch (4-cm) lengths

1 cup (8 fl oz/250 ml) chicken stock

1½ teaspoons cornstarch

2 tablespoons peanut oil

½ red bell pepper (capsicum), seeded,
   deribbed and cut into strips 1½ inches
   (4 cm) long and ¼ inch (6 mm) wide

6 green (spring) onions, including
   2 inches (5 cm) of the tender green
   tops, slivered lengthwise and then cut
   into 1½-inch (4-cm) lengths, plus
   slivered green onions for garnish

2–3 teaspoons dry sherry or Chinese
   rice wine

1–2 tablespoons soy sauce

Serve this spicy Chinese-inspired dish with noodles or steamed white rice. Chinese long beans (available in well stocked food stores and Asian markets) are similar to regular green beans, but are 12 inches (30 cm) long or longer. If neither bean is desired, you may substitute broccoli florets, sliced carrots or asparagus. Toasted sesame seeds are another attractive garnish that can be used with or in place of the green onions.

※

In a bowl, combine the shrimp, garlic, cayenne, ginger, vinegar and sesame oil. Mix well, cover and refrigerate for 1 hour.

Fill a saucepan three-fourths full of water and bring to a boil. Add the beans and boil until almost tender, 4–5 minutes. Drain and let cool. Set aside.

In a small bowl, whisk together the chicken stock and cornstarch until the cornstarch dissolves. Set aside.

In a wok or a large, deep frying pan over high heat, warm the peanut oil until ripples form on the surface. Add the shrimp and its marinade and the bell pepper and toss and stir until the shrimp begin to turn pink, about 2 minutes.

Stir the stock-cornstarch mixture and add it to the pan along with the green beans, 6 green onions, and sherry or rice wine. Toss and stir until the sauce thickens slightly, about 1 minute. Season to taste with the soy sauce.

Transfer to a warmed platter or individual serving dishes, garnish with green onions and serve immediately.

Serves 6

Saffron Rice with Shrimp, Scallops and Roasted Peppers

try

1 small red bell pepper (capsicum)
1 small green bell pepper (capsicum)
1 small yellow bell pepper (capsicum)
¼ cup (2 fl oz/60 ml) olive oil
1 large yellow onion, minced
4 cloves garlic, minced
1½ cups (10½ oz/330 g) short-grain
  white rice
3 tablespoons chopped fresh parsley
½ cup (4 fl oz/125 ml) dry white wine
3 cups (24 fl oz/750 ml) chicken stock
  or fish stock or quick fish stock
  (recipes on pages 12–13)
1½ cups (9 oz/280 g) peeled, halved,
  seeded and chopped tomatoes
  (fresh or canned)
¾ teaspoon saffron threads, steeped in
  1 tablespoon hot water for 10 minutes
½ teaspoon ground turmeric
1 teaspoon salt
½ teaspoon freshly ground pepper
1 lb (500 g) medium shrimp (prawns),
  peeled and deveined
1 lb (500 g) sea or bay scallops
1 lemon, cut into wedges

Saffron is one of the world's most prized spices. Each red-gold thread, the stigma of a crocus variety, must be hand-picked and carefully dried. Saffron's faint, slightly bitter taste marries well with seafood, a combination enjoyed around the Mediterranean.

✳

*P*reheat a broiler (griller).

Cut the bell peppers in half lengthwise and remove the stems, seeds and ribs. Place the peppers, cut side down, on a baking sheet. Broil (grill) until blackened and blistered, 6–10 minutes. Transfer to a plastic or paper bag, close tightly and let steam and cool for 10 minutes. Using your fingers or a small knife, peel off the skin. Cut the peppers into ½-inch (12-mm) dice.

Preheat an oven to 325°F (165°C).

In an ovenproof frying pan or a paella pan about 12 inches (30 cm) in diameter, warm the olive oil over medium heat. Add the onion and garlic and sauté, stirring, until soft, about 10 minutes. Add the rice and parsley and cook, stirring, until the rice is evenly coated with oil, about 2 minutes. Add the bell peppers, wine, stock, tomatoes, saffron and water, turmeric, salt and ground pepper. Boil gently, uncovered, for 5 minutes.

Bury the shrimp and scallops in the rice. Place in the oven and bake, uncovered, for 10 minutes. Cover and continue to bake until the rice is tender and the seafood is cooked, about 10 minutes longer. Remove from the oven and let stand for 10 minutes.

Garnish with lemon wedges and serve.

Serves 6

Jumbo Shrimp Stuffed with Capers, Lemon and Parmesan

6 tablespoons (3 fl oz/90 ml) pure
   olive oil
¼ cup (1½ oz/45 g) minced yellow
   onion
3 cloves garlic, chopped
¾ cup (1½ oz/45 g) fresh bread crumbs
¼ cup (2 oz/60 g) drained capers,
   chopped
⅓ cup (1½ oz/45 g) freshly grated
   Parmesan or pecorino cheese
1½ teaspoons grated lemon zest
1½ tablespoons chopped fresh parsley
1 egg, well beaten
salt and freshly ground pepper
⅓ cup (3 fl oz/80 ml) extra-virgin
   olive oil
3 tablespoons fresh lemon juice
½ teaspoon chopped fresh oregano
½ teaspoon chopped fresh thyme
18 jumbo shrimp (prawns), 1½–2 lb
   (750 g–1 kg) total weight, peeled
   with the tail shells intact and deveined
lemon wedges

This Italian-inspired stuffing for shrimp can be embellished by adding about 3 tablespoons thinly sliced sun-dried tomatoes or sautéed sliced mushrooms or fennel. If you like, serve the shrimp with a green salad dressed with a lemon or orange vinaigrette.

❈

In a frying pan over medium heat, warm 4 tablespoons (2 fl oz/60 ml) of the pure olive oil. Add the onion and sauté, stirring, until soft, about 7 minutes. Add the garlic and sauté for 2 minutes. Add the bread crumbs and stir over low heat for 30 seconds. Transfer to a bowl. Add the capers, cheese, 1 teaspoon of the lemon zest, 1 tablespoon of the parsley and the egg. Mix well and season to taste with salt and pepper.

In another bowl, whisk together the extra-virgin olive oil, lemon juice, the remaining ½ teaspoon lemon zest, the oregano, thyme, the remaining ½ tablespoon parsley and salt and pepper to taste. Set aside.

Starting at the tail end, cut a long pocket along the inside edge of each shrimp, stopping just short of the head end. Press as much filling as possible into the pocket. Cover and refrigerate until ready to cook.

Preheat a broiler (griller).

Brush the shrimp lightly with the remaining 2 tablespoons pure olive oil. Place in a single layer on an oiled broiling pan. Broil (grill), turning once, until firm to the touch, 2–2½ minutes on each side.

Place the shrimp on a platter and drizzle with the dressing. Garnish with lemon wedges and serve hot.

Serves 6

w Squash ?
coleslaw
last meal!

Chinese Noodles with Curried Scallops

10-11-04
great
Pat Mallory

1 lb (500 g) sea or bay scallops

1 tablespoon dry sherry or Chinese rice wine

½ teaspoon chili oil

2 tablespoons soy sauce, plus soy sauce to taste

2 teaspoons cornstarch

1 lb (500 g) Chinese egg noodles (fresh; dried; or thawed, frozen)

4 tablespoons (2 fl oz/60 ml) peanut oil

1 yellow onion, thinly sliced

2 cloves garlic, minced

½ lb (250 g) asparagus, trimmed, cut on the diagonal into 1-inch (2.5-cm) pieces, parboiled in water to cover for 3 minutes, drained and cooled

½ cup (4 fl oz/125 ml) chicken stock or fish stock or quick fish stock *(recipes on pages 12–13)* or bottled clam juice

2 teaspoons curry powder

4 green (spring) onions, including 2 inches (5 cm) of the tender green tops, cut on the diagonal into 1-inch (2.5-cm) pieces

¾ cup (3 oz/90 g) bean sprouts

If you cannot find Chinese egg noodles, substitute dried spaghetti, linguine or fedelini. Garnish this flavorful dish with toasted sesame seeds or cilantro (fresh coriander) leaves.

＊

*I*f you are using sea scallops, cut them in half horizontally. If using bay scallops, leave them whole. In a bowl, combine the scallops, sherry or rice wine, chili oil, the 2 tablespoons soy sauce and the cornstarch. Toss to mix well. Let marinate for 1 hour.

Fill a large pot three-fourths full of salted water and bring to a boil. Add the noodles and cook, stirring occasionally, until al dente, 2 minutes for fresh or thawed, frozen noodles or 4–5 minutes for dried noodles. Drain, place in a bowl and toss with 1 tablespoon of the peanut oil. Let cool.

Drain the scallops, reserving the marinade. In a wok or deep frying pan over medium-high heat, warm 1 tablespoon of the peanut oil until ripples form on the surface. Add the scallops and stir and toss until firm to the touch, 2–3 minutes. Transfer the scallops to a bowl. Add the remaining 2 table-spoons peanut oil to the pan and warm until ripples form on the surface. Add the yellow onion, garlic and asparagus and stir and toss until the asparagus is tender-crisp, 2–3 minutes.

Add the reserved noodles and marinade, stock or clam juice, scallops, curry powder, green onions and bean sprouts and stir and toss until heated through and the liquid has thickened slightly. Season to taste with soy sauce.

Place on a warmed platter and serve immediately.

Serves 6

Biscuit-Topped Shellfish Pot Pie

1 lb (500 g) mussels in the shell, debearded and well scrubbed

1 lb (500 g) clams in the shell, well scrubbed

½ cup (4 fl oz/125 ml) dry white wine

1 lb (500 g) large shrimp (prawns), peeled and deveined

1 lb (500 g) sea scallops, cut in half horizontally

3 tablespoons unsalted butter

6 tablespoons (2 oz/60 g) all-purpose (plain) flour

3 cups (24 fl oz/750 ml) fish stock or quick fish stock (*recipes on pages 12–13*) or bottled clam juice

salt and freshly ground pepper

1 cup (5 oz/155 g) fresh or frozen green peas, parboiled in boiling water for 1 minute and drained

1 carrot, peeled, cut into ¼-inch (6-mm) dice, parboiled in boiling water for 3–4 minutes and drained

¾ lb (375 g) fresh button mushrooms, halved and sautéed in 1 tablespoon unsalted butter for 3 minutes

½ teaspoon chopped fresh thyme

FOR THE BUTTERMILK BISCUITS:

2½ cups (12½ oz/390 g) all-purpose (plain) flour

1 teaspoon salt

1 tablespoon baking powder

½ cup (4 oz/125 g) unsalted butter, at room temperature, cut into small pieces

1 cup (8 fl oz/250 ml) buttermilk, at room temperature

Discard any mussels or clams that do not close to the touch. In a large frying pan, bring the wine to a boil. Add the mussels and clams, cover and cook, shaking the pan periodically, until they open, 2–5 minutes. Using a slotted spoon, transfer to a bowl. Remove the meats. Discard the shells and any unopened mussels or clams.

Add the shrimp and scallops to the same pan, cover and simmer over medium heat until the shrimp are pink and the scallops are almost firm, about 2 minutes. Using a slotted spoon, add to the other shellfish. Drain off any liquid in the bowl and set it aside with any pan juices.

In a saucepan over medium heat, melt the butter. Whisk in the flour and cook, stirring, until bubbly, about 2 minutes. Slowly whisk in the stock or clam juice and reserved cooking liquid and cook, stirring, until thickened, about 5 minutes. Season to taste with salt and pepper. Remove from the heat and stir in the shellfish, peas, carrot, mushrooms and thyme. Place in a 1½-qt (1.5-l) oval baking dish about 7–8 inches (18–20 cm) in diameter or 6 by 8 inches (15 by 20 cm). Preheat an oven to 400°F (200°C).

To make the biscuits, in a bowl, sift together the flour, salt and baking powder. Rub in the butter with your fingers to form a coarse meal. Add the buttermilk and mix with a fork until the mixture holds together. Form into a ball and, on a well-floured surface, roll out into a round ½ inch (12 mm) thick. Fold in half and roll it out again. Fold in half again and roll out ½ inch (12 mm) thick. Using a biscuit cutter 2 inches (5 cm) in diameter, cut out 12 biscuits and place on top of the seafood mixture.

Bake until the biscuits are golden and the stew is bubbling, 20–25 minutes. Serve immediately.

Serves 6–8

Cracked Crab with Three Sauces

FOR THE TANGERINE BUTTER:
¾ cup (6 oz/180 g) unsalted butter
3 tablespoons fresh tangerine juice
½ teaspoon grated tangerine zest
1 tablespoon Dijon mustard
salt and freshly ground pepper

FOR THE DILL–GREEN ONION VINAIGRETTE:
3–4 tablespoons fresh lemon juice
1 clove garlic, minced
½ cup (4 fl oz/125 ml) extra-virgin
   olive oil
salt and freshly ground pepper
2 tablespoons chopped fresh dill
¼ cup (¾ oz/20 g) thinly sliced green
   (spring) onions, including 2 inches
   (5 cm) of the tender green tops

1 cup (8 fl oz/250 ml) rémoulade sauce
   (recipe on page 64)

4 qt (4 l) water or court bouillon
   (recipe on page 13)
salt
3 live Dungeness crabs, 2–2½ lb
   (1–1.25 kg) each

A plate of cracked crab is simple to prepare and always satisfying. If you are short of time, you can buy fresh cooked and cracked crab at your local fishmonger. Blue or stone crabs can be used if Dungeness crabs are unavailable; adjust cooking time as necessary.

❋

To make the tangerine butter, in a small saucepan over medium heat, melt the butter. Stir in the tangerine juice and zest, mustard and salt and pepper to taste. Immediately remove from the heat and let stand for 1 hour.

To make the vinaigrette, in a small bowl, whisk together the lemon juice, garlic, olive oil and salt and pepper to taste. Stir in the dill and green onions, mixing well. Set aside.

In a small bowl, make the rémoulade sauce. Cover and refrigerate until serving.

In a stockpot, bring the water or court bouillon to a boil. If using water, add 2 tablespoons salt once it boils. Add the crabs, immersing completely, and boil until cooked, about 12 minutes. Using tongs, transfer to a plate to cool slightly.

Working with 1 crab at a time, place the crab on its back. Pull off the tail section and discard; the intestinal vein will pull free at the same time. Then turn the crab over and, grasping the large top shell firmly, lift it, snap it off and discard. Remove the white spongy gills and any other organs from the body and discard. Using a large, heavy knife, cut the body in half from head to tail. Cut each half crosswise into thirds. Using a mallet, crack the claws and legs. If the crabs have cooled, warm them on a steamer rack over boiling water for 5–7 minutes.

To serve, reheat the tangerine butter over medium heat, whisking constantly. Pour into a small bowl. Arrange the crab on a platter. Serve immediately with the sauces.

Serves 6

Fettuccine with Shrimp, Parmesan and Avocado Cream

1½ lb (750 g) dried fettuccine

3 tablespoons olive oil

1 lb (500 g) large shrimp (prawns), peeled and deveined

3 tablespoons chopped fresh parsley

3 cloves garlic, minced

½ fresh red or green jalapeño chili pepper, seeded and minced

¼ cup (2 fl oz/60 ml) dry white wine

1½ cups (12 fl oz/375 ml) heavy (double) cream

2 avocados, halved, pitted, peeled and cut into ½-inch (12-mm) dice

1 cup (4 oz/125 g) freshly grated Parmesan cheese

4 tablespoons chopped fresh cilantro (fresh coriander)

1–2 teaspoons fresh lime juice

salt and freshly ground pepper

The robust country flavors of the American Southwest are subtly portrayed in this delicious pasta dish. Linguine, spaghetti, fusilli or small shells can be substituted for the fettuccine, and bay scallops can be used in place of the shrimp. If desired, garnish with lime wedges and cilantro sprigs.

❋

*F*ill a large pot three-fourths full of salted water and bring to a boil. Add the pasta and cook until al dente, 10–12 minutes, or according to the timing on the package.

Meanwhile, in a frying pan over medium heat, warm the olive oil. Add the shrimp and cook, stirring, until pink and curled slightly, 1½ minutes. Add the parsley, garlic and chili pepper and cook, stirring, for 30 seconds.

Raise the heat to high, add the wine and cook until reduced by half, about 30 seconds. Add the cream and cook until reduced by one-fourth, about 1 minute. Remove from the heat and add the avocado, Parmesan cheese, cilantro, lime juice and salt and pepper to taste.

When the pasta is done, drain and transfer to a warmed platter. Pour the sauce over the top, toss well and serve.

Serves 6

Sesame Seed–Crusted Scallops

½ cup (2½ oz/75 g) all-purpose (plain)
  flour
3 eggs
2 cups (8 oz/250 g) sesame seeds
1 teaspoon kosher salt
¼ teaspoon freshly ground pepper
1½ lb (750 g) sea scallops
3 tablespoons unsalted butter
orange wedges
fresh parsley leaves, preferably flat-leaf
  (Italian)

This recipe can also be made with peeled large shrimp (prawns). Accompany it with your favorite homemade coleslaw, adding a little of the Japanese green horseradish called wasabi or regular creamed horseradish to the dressing to give it some heat.

✺

*P*lace the flour in a bowl. Whisk the eggs together well in another bowl. In yet another bowl, stir together the sesame seeds, kosher salt and the pepper.

Dip the scallops, a few at a time, into the flour and shake off the excess. Then dip the scallops into the beaten egg and finally into the sesame seeds, turning to coat completely.

In a large frying pan over medium heat, melt the butter. Add the scallops and fry, turning once, until golden on both sides and opaque in the center, 3–4 minutes.

Transfer the scallops to a warmed platter and garnish with orange wedges and parsley leaves. Serve immediately.

Serves 6

Grilled Lobster with Citrus Butter

4 qt (4 l) water or court bouillon
   (recipe on page 13)
salt
6 live lobsters, 1½ lb (750 g) each
½ cup (4 oz/125 g) plus 2 tablespoons
   unsalted butter, at room temperature
¼ teaspoon grated lemon zest
¼ teaspoon grated lime zest
¼ teaspoon grated orange zest
2 tablespoons chopped fresh parsley
½ teaspoon dried herbes de Provence
freshly ground pepper

Dousing the embers with water gives the finished lobster a pleasantly smoky flavor. To offer this dish as a first course, split one lobster for two people. If you like, garnish with citrus wedges and sprigs of flat-leaf (Italian) parsley. Provide plenty of lobster crackers or nut crackers for cracking the heavy lobster claws.

❋

*I*n a large stockpot, bring the water or court bouillon to a boil. If using water, add 2 tablespoons salt once it reaches a boil. Add 2 lobsters, immersing completely, and boil until the shells turn red, about 4 minutes. Using tongs, remove the lobsters and place under cold running water to cool. Repeat with the remaining lobsters, two at a time.

Prepare a fire in a charcoal grill.

Lay a lobster, underside down, on a cutting board. Insert a knife into the lobster at the point where the body meets the tail and cut the tail in half lengthwise. Turn the lobster around and cut toward the head, cutting the lobster into two pieces. Remove the black intestinal vein and any other organs and discard.

In a small saucepan over medium heat, melt the butter and stir in the lemon, lime and orange zest, parsley, herbes de Provence, and salt and pepper to taste. Remove from the heat.

Place the lobsters on the grill rack, cut side up. Cover with the grill top or a large inverted metal bowl and cook for 2 minutes. Pour ½ cup (4 fl oz/125 ml) water over the coals to create smoke and continue to cook, covered, for 2 minutes. Remove the cover and drizzle the lobsters with half of the citrus butter. Re-cover and cook until the meat is almost firm to the touch, about 2 minutes.

Transfer the lobsters to a platter, cut side up, and drizzle with the remaining citrus butter. Serve hot.

Serves 6

Lobster and Champagne Risotto

6 cups (48 fl oz/1.5 l) water or court
   bouillon (recipe on page 13)
salt
2 live lobsters, about 1¼ lb (625 g) each
3 cups (24 fl oz/750 ml) dry
   Champagne or sparkling wine
3 tablespoons unsalted butter
1 large yellow onion, minced
1½ cups (10½ oz/330 g) Arborio rice
4 tablespoons chopped fresh chives,
   plus whole fresh chives for garnish
2 tablespoons chopped fresh parsley
½–1 teaspoon fresh lemon juice
½ cup (4 fl oz/125 ml) heavy (double)
   cream
freshly ground pepper

If you like, substitute one 2–2½ pound (1–1.25 kg) live Dungeness crab for the lobsters and dry white wine for the Champagne.

❋

*I*n a stockpot, bring the water or court bouillon to a boil. If using water, add 2 teaspoons salt once it reaches a boil. Add the lobsters, immersing completely, and cook until dark red and fully cooked, about 10 minutes. Using tongs, lift out the lobsters and let cool. Reserve the cooking liquid.

   Remove the lobster meat from the shells as directed on page 8. Discard the tomalley, black intestinal vein and any other organs. Dice the meat; set aside. Add the shells to the cooking liquid and reduce the liquid over high heat to 3 cups (24 fl oz/750 ml). This should take about 15 minutes. Strain through a fine-mesh sieve lined with cheesecloth (muslin) into a saucepan; add the Champagne or other sparkling wine. Bring to a simmer.

   In a frying pan over medium heat, melt the butter. Add the onion and sauté, stirring, until very soft, about 12 minutes. Add the rice and continue to stir over medium heat until transparent, 3–4 minutes. Add about ½ cup (4 fl oz/125 ml) of the simmering liquid and stir continuously, scraping the rice away from the bottom and sides of the pan. When the liquid has been almost completely absorbed, add another ½ cup (4 fl oz/125 ml) liquid, stirring continuously. Continue in this manner, keeping the grains slightly moist at all times, until the rice is firm but tender and does not have a chalky center, 20–25 minutes. (If you run out of liquid before the rice is ready, add hot water.)

   To the cooked rice mixture, add a final ½ cup (4 fl oz/125 ml) simmering liquid or hot water, the lobster meat, chopped chives, parsley, lemon juice, cream, and salt and pepper to taste. Stir over low heat to combine the ingredients. Transfer to a platter, garnish with whole chives and serve immediately.

Serves 6

Spicy Clam Ragout with Garlic Mashed Potatoes

salt

1½ lb (750 g) red potatoes, peeled and quartered

½ cup (2 oz/60 g) peeled whole garlic cloves, plus 3 large garlic cloves, minced

1 fennel bulb

3 tablespoons extra-virgin olive oil

2 yellow onions, thinly sliced

1 teaspoon ground fennel seeds

¼ teaspoon red pepper flakes

1 cup (8 fl oz/250 ml) dry white wine

1½ cups (9 oz/280 g) drained canned tomatoes, crushed

3 lb (1.5 kg) clams, well scrubbed

1 lb (500 g) hot Italian sausages, simmered in ¼ cup (2 fl oz/60 ml) water for 5 minutes, turning once, then cut on the diagonal into slices ½ inch (12 mm) thick

freshly ground pepper

¼ cup (2 fl oz/60 ml) heavy (double) cream, warmed slightly

4 tablespoons coarsely chopped fresh parsley

For a mild dish, use sweet Italian sausage and omit the pepper flakes.

✻

*F*ill a saucepan three-fourths full of water and bring to a boil. Add salt to taste, the potatoes and whole garlic cloves and boil until the potatoes are tender when pierced, about 30 minutes. Drain the potatoes and garlic, cover and keep warm.

Meanwhile, cut off the stems and feathery tops of the fennel and reserve for another use. Discard any tough outer leaves from the bulb. Using a sharp knife, thinly slice the bulb lengthwise.

In a large frying pan over medium heat, warm the olive oil. Add the fennel, onions, minced garlic, ground fennel seeds and red pepper flakes. Cover and cook, stirring occasionally, until the vegetables are very soft, about 15 minutes. Raise the heat to high and add the wine. Cook, uncovered, for 3 minutes. Add the tomatoes, reduce the heat to medium-low and simmer, stirring occasionally, until thickened, about 15 minutes.

Discard any clams that do not close to the touch. Add the clams and sausage to the tomato mixture, cover and cook until the clams open, about 5 minutes. Uncover and simmer until the tomato mixture thickens slightly, 3–4 minutes. Discard any unopened clams. Season with salt and pepper.

Pass the potatoes and garlic through a potato ricer or a food mill placed over a bowl (or mash with a potato masher). Add the cream and salt and pepper to taste.

To serve, place the potatoes in the center of a serving plate. Spoon the ragout around the potatoes and garnish with the parsley.

Serves 6

Crab Soufflé Baked in 10 Minutes

Make sure your dinner guests are already seated when you remove this dramatic dish from the oven, then place it in the center of the table so they can admire it before serving.

✳

6 tablespoons (3 oz/90 g) unsalted butter

1½ cups (12 fl oz/375 ml) milk

1 cup (8 fl oz/250 ml) heavy (double) cream

¼ cup (1 oz/30 g) minced green (spring) onions, including tender green tops

5 tablespoons (1¾ oz/50 g) all-purpose (plain) flour

5 egg yolks

¾ cup (3 oz/90 g) freshly grated Parmesan cheese

1 teaspoon dry mustard

½ teaspoon chopped fresh thyme or ¼ teaspoon dried thyme

pinch of cayenne pepper

1 tablespoon fresh lemon juice

salt and freshly ground pepper

6 egg whites

½ lb (250 g) fresh cooked crab meat, picked over for shell fragments and cartilage

Position a rack in the top part of an oven and preheat the oven to 450°F (230°C). Butter a rimmed ovenproof platter about 18 inches (45 cm) long and 10 inches (25 cm) wide with 1 tablespoon of the butter.

Pour the milk and cream into a saucepan and place over low heat. Warm until small bubbles form along the edge of the pan. In another saucepan over medium heat, melt the remaining 5 tablespoons (2½ oz/75 g) butter. Add the green onions and sauté, stirring, for 2 minutes. Using a whisk, stir in the flour and continue to cook, stirring, until the mixture bubbles, about 2 minutes. Slowly add the cream mixture while stirring rapidly with a whisk. Then cook, stirring, until thick and smooth, 2–3 minutes.

Remove from the heat and whisk in the egg yolks, one at a time, whisking well after each addition. Add half of the Parmesan cheese, the mustard, thyme, cayenne, lemon juice and salt and pepper to taste. Mix well.

In a bowl, beat the egg whites until stiff, glossy peaks form. Stir one-half of the egg whites into the cheese sauce to lighten it, then gently fold in the remaining egg whites and the crab meat. Immediately pour the mixture onto the prepared platter and sprinkle the top with the remaining cheese.

Bake on the top rack of the oven until golden brown, about 10 minutes. Serve immediately.

Serves 6

Fusilli with Mussels, Tomatoes and Orange

2 lb (1 kg) mussels, debearded and well
  scrubbed
¼ cup (2 fl oz/60 ml) dry white wine
2 tablespoons extra-virgin olive oil
1 large red (Spanish) onion, thinly
  sliced
3 cloves garlic, minced
4 large tomatoes, diced
⅓ cup (3 fl oz/80 ml) fresh orange juice
½ teaspoon grated orange zest
pinch of red pepper flakes, optional
salt and freshly ground pepper
1 lb (500 g) dried fusilli
½ cup (½ oz/15 g) fresh basil leaves,
  finely shredded

A chunky tomato sauce flavored with orange juice and a hint of spicy red pepper has its origins in the cooking of southern Italy. Substitute clams for the mussels, if you prefer. Rigatoni, shells, penne, linguine or fettuccine can be used in place of the fusilli.

❋

Fill a large pot three-fourths full of salted water and bring to a boil. Discard any mussels that do not close to the touch.

In a large frying pan over high heat, warm the wine. Add the mussels, cover and cook, shaking the pan periodically, until the mussels open, 2–4 minutes. Transfer the mussels and their juices to a bowl and set aside.

In the same pan over medium heat, warm the olive oil. Add the onion and sauté until soft, about 10 minutes. Add the garlic and continue to sauté for 2 minutes. Add the tomatoes, orange juice, orange zest, red pepper flakes (if using) and salt and pepper to taste. Simmer uncovered for 3 minutes.

While the sauce is cooking, add the pasta to the boiling water and cook until al dente, about 12 minutes, or according to the timing on the package.

Discard any unopened mussels, then add the mussels and their juices to the sauce. Simmer uncovered until heated through.

As soon as the pasta is ready, drain and place on a warmed platter. Pour the sauce over the top, toss and garnish with the shredded basil. Serve immediately.

Serves 6

Cioppino with Clams, Shrimp and Crab

2 Dungeness crabs, cooked

¼ cup (2 fl oz/60 ml) olive oil

1 large yellow onion, chopped

1 small green bell pepper (capsicum),
   seeded, deribbed and cut into ½-inch
   (12-mm) dice

4 cloves garlic, minced

1 lb (500 g) red snapper or rock cod
   fillets, cut into 1-inch (2.5-cm) pieces

1 cup (8 fl oz/250 ml) dry white wine

2 cups (16 fl oz/500 ml) fish stock or
   quick fish stock (recipes on pages 12–13)
   or bottled clam juice

2 cups (16 fl oz/500 ml) water

2½ cups (15 oz/470 g) peeled, halved,
   seeded and chopped tomatoes
   (fresh or canned)

1 tablespoon tomato paste

2 bay leaves

½ teaspoon dried basil

pinch of red pepper flakes

salt and freshly ground pepper

1 lb (500 g) clams, well scrubbed

1 lb (500 g) large shrimp (prawns)

3 tablespoons chopped fresh parsley

San Francisco's simple shellfish-and-fish stew, called cioppino, recalls the seafood stews found along the Mediterranean coast. It pairs well with another San Francisco culinary tradition, sourdough bread. Stone crab claws and blue crabs can be used in place of Dungeness. Mussels can replace the clams, and scallops can be substituted for the shrimp.

※

Clean and crack the crabs and remove the meat as directed on page 9, reserving any juices. Discard the shells.

In a soup pot over medium heat, warm the olive oil. Add the onion, bell pepper and garlic and sauté, stirring, until soft, about 7 minutes. Add the crab meat, crab juices and fish fillets and cook slowly uncovered, stirring occasionally, for 10 minutes. Raise the heat to high, add the wine and cook for 2 minutes. Reduce the heat to medium and gently stir in the fish stock or clam juice, the water, tomatoes, tomato paste, bay leaves, basil, red pepper flakes and salt and pepper to taste. Simmer, uncovered, for 10 minutes.

Discard any clams that do not close to the touch. Add the clams and simmer until they open, 3–5 minutes. Discard any unopened clams. Add the shrimp and continue to simmer until firm to the touch, 3–4 minutes. Adjust the seasoning with salt and pepper and remove from the heat.

To serve, ladle into warmed bowls and garnish with the parsley. Serve immediately.

Serves 6

Shrimp Jambalaya

¼ cup (2 oz/60 g) bacon drippings or
  (2 fl oz/60 ml) vegetable oil
1 lb (500 g) lean cooked ham, cut into
  ½-inch (12-mm) cubes
2 yellow onions, finely chopped
1 small green bell pepper (capsicum),
  seeded, deribbed and chopped
2 celery stalks, chopped
4 cloves garlic, minced
1 can (28 oz/875 g) plum (Roma)
  tomatoes, drained, juices reserved,
  and chopped
4 tablespoons chopped fresh parsley
½ teaspoon chopped fresh thyme
1 teaspoon salt
freshly ground pepper
4 cups (32 fl oz/1 l) chicken stock or
  fish stock or quick fish stock
  (recipes on pages 12–13)
1½ cups (10½ oz/330 g) long-grain
  white rice
1½ lb (750 g) medium shrimp (prawns),
  peeled and deveined
hot-pepper sauce, such as Tabasco

In the Cajun and Creole country of the American South, there are countless versions of this venerable one-dish meal. Some jambalayas are hearty, some light, some mild and some spicy hot. If you like it hot and can locate andouille sausage, a type of smoked pork sausage, thinly slice about ½ pound (500 g) of it and add in place of half of the ham.

✳

*I*n a soup pot over medium heat, warm the bacon drippings or vegetable oil. Add the ham and sauté, stirring, until browned on all sides, 15–20 minutes.

Add the onions, bell pepper, celery and garlic and sauté over medium heat, stirring, until the onions are soft, about 7 minutes. Add the tomatoes and their juices, parsley, thyme, 1 teaspoon salt and pepper to taste and simmer, uncovered, for 5 minutes. Add the stock and rice, cover tightly and cook over low heat until the rice is tender, about 20 minutes.

Uncover, add the shrimp and stir well. Continue to cook for 2 minutes. Remove from the heat and let stand, covered, for 10 minutes.

Spoon the jambalaya onto a platter and pass the hot-pepper sauce at the table.

Serves 6

Glossary

The following glossary defines terms both generally and specifically as they relate to shellfish, including major and unusual ingredients and basic techniques.

ANCHOVIES

Tiny saltwater fish, related to sardines. Imported anchovy fillets packed in olive oil in cans are the most commonly available; anchovies packed in salt, available canned in some Italian delicatessens, are considered the best.

AVOCADO

The finest-flavored variety of this popular vegetable-fruit is the Hass, which has a pearlike shape and a thick, bumpy, dark green skin. Ripe, ready-to-use avocados will yield slightly to fingertip pressure.

BAGUETTE

Traditional long, narrow French-style bread loaf, usually about 2 feet (60 cm) in length and no more than about 4 inches (10 cm) in diameter.

BAY LEAVES

Dried whole leaves of the bay laurel tree. Pungent and spicy, they flavor simmered dishes, marinades and pickling mixtures. The French variety, sometimes available in specialty-food shops, has a milder, sweeter flavor than California bay leaves. Discard the leaves before serving.

BELL PEPPER

Fresh, sweet-fleshed, bell-shaped member of the pepper family. Also known as capsicum. Most common in the unripe green form, although ripened red or yellow varieties are also available. Creamy pale-yellow, orange and purple-black types may also be found.

To prepare a raw bell pepper, cut it in half lengthwise with a sharp knife. Pull out the stem section from each half, along with the cluster of seeds attached to it.

Remove any remaining seeds, along with any thin white membranes, or ribs, to which they are attached.

Cut the pepper halves into quarters, strips or thin slices, as called for in the specific recipe.

BREAD CRUMBS

For good bread crumbs, choose a high-quality, rustic-style loaf with a firm, coarse-textured crumb. For fresh crumbs, cut away the crusts from the bread and break the bread into coarse chunks. Put them in a food processor fitted with the metal blade or in a blender and process to desired consistency. For dried crumbs, spread the bread crumbs in a baking pan and leave in an oven set at its lowest temperature until they feel very dry, 30–60 minutes; do not let brown.

CAPERS

Small, pickled buds of a bush common to the Mediterranean, used whole as a savory flavoring or garnish.

CAYENNE PEPPER

Very hot ground spice derived from dried cayenne chili peppers.

CHILI OIL

Popular seasoning of sesame or vegetable oil in which hot chilies have been steeped. Available in Asian markets and the specialty-food section of most food stores.

CHILIES

A wide variety of fresh chilies may be found in well-stocked markets. Two common types are used in this book.

The jalapeño (below) is a small, thick-fleshed, very hot chili that is usually sold green, although red ripened specimens may sometimes be found.

The serrano (below) is a small, slender, fiery green chili also sold in its ripened red form or pickled in brine.

The seeds and white ribs found inside a chili are intensely hot, and may be removed before the chili is used.

CHINESE LONG BEANS

Asian variety of green bean (below) commonly measuring 1 foot (30 cm) or more in length. Available in Chinese markets and well-stocked vegetable stores. Also known as snake beans.

CHIVES

Mild, sweet herb with a flavor reminiscent of the **onion,** to which it is related. Although chives are available dried in the herb-and-spice section of food stores, fresh chives possess the best flavor.

CILANTRO

Green, leafy herb resembling flat-leaf (Italian) **parsley,** with a sharp, aromatic, somewhat astringent flavor. Popular in Latin American and Asian cuisines. Also called fresh coriander and commonly referred to as Chinese parsley.

CLAM JUICE

The strained liquid of shucked clams, sold in small bottles in the fresh or canned seafood departments of food stores. Because of its refreshing briny flavor, the juice is often used as a cooking liquid for seafood dishes.

CORNSTARCH

Fine, powdery flour ground from the endosperm of corn—the white heart of the kernel—and used as a neutral-flavored thickening agent. Also known as cornflour.

CREAM, HEAVY

Whipping cream with a butterfat content of at least 36 percent. For the best flavor and cooking properties, purchase 100 percent natural fresh cream with a short shelf life printed on the carton, avoiding long-lasting varieties that have been processed by ultraheat methods. In Britain, use double cream.

FAVA BEAN
Variety of fresh or dried bean resembling an oversized lima bean. Fresh fava beans are sold in their long, plump, flattened pods, and are easily shelled; many cooks also peel off the tough but edible skin that encases each bean. Also known as broad bean.

FENNEL
Crisp, refreshing, mildly anise-flavored bulb vegetable, sometimes called by its Italian name, *finocchio*. Another related variety of the bulb is valued for its fine, feathery leaves and stems, which are used as a fresh or dried herb, and for its small, crescent-shaped seeds, dried and used whole or ground as a spice.

FETTUCCINE
Long, flat ribbons of fresh or dried pasta, about ¼ inch (6 mm) wide.

FISH SAUCE
Popular Southeast Asian seasoning prepared from salted, fermented fish, usually **anchovies.** Available in Asian markets and specialty-food sections of well-stocked food stores. Known variously as *nuoc mam* (Vietnamese), *nam pla* (Thai) and *patis* (Filipino).

FONTINA
Firm, creamy, mild-tasting Italian cheese made from sheep's milk.

FUSILLI
Thin, spindly dried pasta shapes resembling coiled fuses.

GARLIC
Pungent bulb popular worldwide as a flavoring ingredient, both raw and cooked. To peel a garlic clove, place on a work surface and cover with the side of a large chef's knife. Press down firmly on the side of the knife to crush the clove slightly; the dry skin will then slip off easily.

GINGER
The rhizome of the tropical ginger plant, which yields a sweet, strong-flavored spice. Whole ginger rhizomes (below), commonly but mistakenly called roots, can be purchased fresh in a food store or vegetable market. Before slicing, chopping or grating, the brown, papery skin should be peeled away from the amount being used.

HERBES DE PROVENCE
A mixture of dried herbs typically including **thyme,** rosemary, sage, marjoram, basil, **fennel** and mint.

HORSERADISH
Pungent, hot-tasting root, a member of the mustard family, sold fresh and whole, or already grated and bottled as a prepared sauce. The best prepared horse-radish is the freshly grated variety, bottled in a light **vinegar** and found in the refrigerated section of the food store.

HOT-PEPPER SAUCE
Bottled commercial cooking and table sauce made from fresh or dried hot red chilies. Many varieties are available, but Tabasco is the most commonly known brand.

LEMONGRASS
Thick, stalklike grass with a sharp, lemony flavor, popular in Southeast Asian cooking and available fresh or dried in some Asian food stores. If fresh lemongrass is unavailable, substitute 1 tablespoon dried lemongrass for each 8-inch (20-cm) stalk of fresh; or substitute long, thin strips of lemon peel.

LETTUCE, ROMAINE
Popular variety of lettuce with elongated, pale green leaves characterized by their crisp texture and slightly pungent flavor. Also known as cos lettuce.

MANGO
Tropical fruit with juicy, aromatic orange flesh. Ripe mangoes yield slightly to finger pressure; ripen firm mangoes at room temperature in an open paper or plastic bag. The skin peels easily when slit with a knife. Slice the flesh from both sides of the large, flat pit, as well as from around its edges.

MONTEREY JACK
Semisoft white melting cheese with a mild flavor and buttery texture.

OKRA
Small, mild, slender green vegetable pods, 1½–3 inches (4–7.5 cm) in length, with crisp outer flesh and thick, mucilaginous juices when cooked.

ONIONS
All manner of onions are used to enhance the flavor of shellfish dishes. Green onions, also called

OILS
Oils not only provide a medium in which foods may be browned without sticking, but can also subtly enhance the flavor of recipes in which they are used. Store all oils in airtight containers away from heat and light.

Extra-virgin olive oil, extracted from olives on the first pressing without use of heat or chemicals, is prized for its fruity taste and golden to pale green hue. Many brands, varying in color and strength of flavor, are widely available; choose one that suits your taste. The higher-priced extra-virgin olive oils usually are of better quality. Products labeled *pure olive oil* are less aromatic and flavorful and may be used for all-purpose cooking.

Pale gold *peanut oil* has a subtle hint of the peanut's richness.

Rich, flavorful and aromatic *sesame oil* is pressed from sesame seeds. Sesame oils from China and Japan are made with toasted sesame seeds, resulting in a dark, strong oil used as a flavoring ingredient; their low smoking temperature makes them unsuitable for using alone for cooking. Cold-pressed sesame oil, made from untoasted seeds, is lighter in color and taste, and may be used for cooking.

Bland vegetable and seed oils such as *safflower* and *corn oil* are employed for their high cooking temperatures and mild flavor.

spring onions or scallions, are a variety harvested immature, leaves and all, before their bulbs have formed. The green and white parts may both be enjoyed, raw or cooked, for their mild but still pronounced onion flavor. Red (Spanish) onions are a mild, sweet variety of onion with purplish red skin and red-tinged white flesh. Yellow onions are the common, white-fleshed, strong-flavored variety distinguished by their dry, yellowish brown skins.

OREGANO
Aromatic, pungent and spicy Mediterranean herb—also known as wild marjoram—used fresh or dried as a seasoning for all kinds of savory dishes.

OYSTER CRACKERS
Small, six-sided crackers made primarily of wheat flour, shortening and baking soda (sodium bicarbonate). Noted for their crispness and mild flavor, they are a popular companion to oysters and soup.

PAPAYA
Tropical fruit shaped somewhat like a large pear or **avocado**, with soft, sweet orange flesh—milder tasting than a **mango**—and smooth yellow skin. When ripe, a papaya yields to gentle finger pressure; ripen green papayas in a bowl at room temperature. Halve lengthwise and scoop out the shiny black seeds before peeling. Papayas are most readily available during the spring and summer months.

PAPRIKA
Powdered spice derived from the dried paprika pepper; popular in several European cuisines and available in sweet, mild and hot forms. Hungarian paprika is the best, but Spanish paprika, which is mild, may also be used.

PARMESAN
Hard, thick-crusted Italian cow's milk cheese with a sharp, salty, full flavor resulting from at least two years of aging. Buy in block form, to grate fresh as needed, rather than already grated. The finest Italian variety is designated Parmigiano-Reggiano®.

PARSLEY
This popular fresh herb is available in two varieties: the more popular curly-leaf type and a flat-leaf type (at right). The latter, also known as Italian parsley, has a more pronounced flavor and is preferred.

SHELLFISH
Among the many varieties of shellfish and crustaceans sold in well-stocked seafood markets, the most popular and commonly available, featured in this book, are:

Clams
Bivalve mollusks prized for their sweet, tender flesh. Sold live in their shells, or sometimes already shucked. Discard any clams that do not close tightly upon touching. Once cooked, discard any that did not open.

Crab
Already-cooked crab meat is widely available. Although it is often sold frozen, seek out fresh cooked crab meat for the best flavor and texture. When fresh crab is in season (September–April), fish markets often sell cooked whole crabs; ask for them to be cracked, or crack them yourself and then remove the meat (see page 9).

The shelled meat, particularly from the body of the crab, is known as lump crab meat; finer particles of crab meat, from the legs or broken down from larger lumps, is known as flaked crab meat. Avoid imitation crab meat (surimi).

Lobster
Although many seafood stores and some food markets sell lobsters already cooked, cleaned and shelled, it is usually far more economical, and yields better results, to buy a live lobster and cook it yourself.

Mussels
Before cooking, these popular, bluish black–shelled bivalves require special cleaning to remove any dirt adhering to their shells and to remove their "beards," the fibrous threads by which the mussels connect to rocks or piers in the coastal waters where they live (see page 10).

Oysters
Buy fresh oysters only from a reputable fish market. They vary in size, shape and flavor from area to area. They are available live in the shell as well as shucked and in their liquor.

Scallops
These bivalve mollusks come in two common varieties: the round flesh of sea scallops is usually 1½ inches (4 cm) in diameter, while the bay scallop is considerably smaller. Both are usually sold already shelled.

Shrimp
Raw shrimp (prawns) are generally sold with the heads already removed but the shells still intact. Before cooking they are usually peeled and their thin, veinlike intestinal tracts removed (see page 11).

RADISH
Crisp root vegetable, usually eaten raw and prized for its refreshing flavor characterized by a pungent, peppery hotness that varies from mild to assertive.

RED PEPPER FLAKES
Coarsely ground flakes of dried red chilies, including seeds, which add moderately hot flavor to the foods they season.

RICE, ARBORIO
Popular Italian variety of rice with short, round grains high in starch content, which creates a creamy, saucelike consistency during cooking. Available in Italian delicatessens and well-stocked food stores.

RICE WINE
A popular ingredient and beverage in many Asian countries, made by fermenting rice soaked in water, sometimes together with other grains. Good-quality medium-dry sherry may be substituted. Look for rice wine in Asian food stores.

SAFFRON
Intensely aromatic spice, golden orange in color, made from the dried stigmas of a species of crocus; used to perfume and color many classic Mediterranean and East Indian dishes. Sold either as threads—the dried stigmas— or in powdered form. Look for products labeled pure saffron.

SALTINE CRACKERS
Square, crisp, salted crackers made predominantly of wheat flour, shortening and baking soda—a popular accompaniment to hors d'oeuvres and appetizers. Their crumbs are also used in stuffings and as a coating for fried foods.

SESAME SEEDS
Tiny, pale ivory-colored seeds with a mild, nutty flavor; used most often as a garnish.

SHALLOT
Small member of the **onion** family with brown skin, white-to-purple flesh and a flavor resembling a cross between sweet onion and **garlic.**

SHERRY
Fortified, cask-aged wine, ranging in styles from dry to sweet. Enjoyed as an aperitif and used as a flavoring in both savory and sweet recipes.

SOY SAUCE
Asian seasoning and condiment made from soybeans, wheat, salt and water. Seek out good-quality imported soy sauces; Chinese brands tend to be markedly saltier than Japanese.

TARRAGON
Fragrant, distinctively sweet herb used fresh or dried as a seasoning for salads, seafood, chicken, light meats, eggs and vegetables.

THYME
Fragrant, clean-tasting, small-leaved herb (below) popular fresh or dried as a seasoning for seafood, poultry, light meats or vegetables.

TOMATILLO
Small, green tomatillos resemble but are not related to **tomatoes.**

Fresh tomatillos, available in some Latin American markets and well-stocked food stores, usually come encased in brown papery husks, easily peeled off before tomatillos are cut. Canned tomatillos may be found in specialty-food sections of markets.

TOMATO PASTE
A commercial concentrate of puréed **tomatoes,** used to add flavor and body to sauces. Commonly sold in small cans. Imported tubes of double-strength tomato concentrate, sold in Italian delicatessens and well-stocked food markets, have a superior flavor.

TOMATOES
During summer, when tomatoes are in season, use the best red or yellow vine-ripened tomatoes you can find. At other times of year, plum tomatoes, sometimes called Roma or egg tomatoes, are likely to have the best flavor and texture; for cooking, canned whole plum tomatoes are also good.
  To peel fresh tomatoes, first bring a saucepan of water to a boil. Using a small, sharp knife, cut out the core from the stem end of the tomato. Then cut a shallow X in the skin at the tomato's base. Submerge for about 20 seconds in the boiling water, then remove and dip in a bowl of cold water. Starting at the X, peel the skin from the tomato, using your fingertips and, if necessary, the knife blade. Cut the tomatoes in half and turn each half cut-side down. Then cut as directed in individual recipes.
  To seed a tomato, cut it in half crosswise. Squeeze gently to force out the seed sacs.

VINEGARS
Literally "sour wine," vinegar results when certain strains of yeast cause wine—or some other alcoholic liquid such as apple cider or Japanese rice wine—to ferment for a second time, turning it acidic. The best-quality wine vinegars begin with good-quality wine. Red wine vinegar, like the wine from which it is made, has a more robust flavor than vinegar produced from white wine; vinegar produced from Champagne grapes has a very refined flavor. Balsamic vinegar, a specialty of Modena, Italy, is a vinegar made from reduced grape juice and aged for many years.

ZEST
Thin, brightly colored, outer-most layer of a citrus fruit's peel, containing most of its aromatic essential oils—a lively source of flavor. Zest may be removed using one of two easy methods:

1. Use a simple tool known as a zester, drawing its sharp-edged holes across the fruit's skin to remove the zest in thin strips. Alternatively, use a fine hand-held grater.

2. Holding the edge of a paring knife or vegetable peeler almost parallel to the fruit's skin, carefully cut off the zest in thin strips, taking care not to remove any white pith with it. Then thinly slice or chop on a cutting board.

Index

✻

ACKNOWLEDGMENTS

The publishers would like to thank the following people and organizations for their
generous assistance and support in producing this book:
Jean Tenanes, Anita Anderson, Sharon C. Lott, Stephen W. Griswold, Michelle Syracuse, Ken DellaPenta, Tarji Mickelson,
Jennifer Hauser, Jennifer Mullins, Claire Sanchez, and the buyers and store managers for Pottery Barn and Williams-Sonoma stores.

The following kindly lent props for the photography: Biordi Art Imports, Candelier, Fredericksen Hardware,
Sandra Griswold, Fillamento, Forrest Jones, Sue Fisher King, RH Shop, Waterford/Wedgwood and Chuck Williams.